The Gospel of John

Part 2
Chapters 9-21

William MacDonald

EMMAUS
WORLDWIDE

Developed as a study course by Emmaus Correspondence School, founded in 1942.

The Gospel of John — Part 2
William MacDonald

Published by:
  Emmaus Worldwide
  PO Box 1028
  Dubuque, IA 52004-1028
  phone: (563) 585-2070
  email: info@emmausworldwide.org
  website: www.EmmausWorldwide.org

First Edition 2017 (AK '17), 2 UNITS
Revised 2020 (AK '20), 2 UNITS

ISBN 978-1-59387-149-9

Code: JOHN2

Printed in the United States of America

Course Overview

John the apostle wrote his gospel many years after Matthew, Mark, and Luke had penned theirs. Already, the church was being plagued by error and by attacks upon the person and work of God's beloved Son. So, under the inspiration of the Holy Spirit, John sought to give clear testimony to the deity of Jesus Christ. He concentrates on presenting the miracles and words of Jesus and then interpreting them for his readers. His goal? That you, the reader, "… may believe that Jesus is the Christ, the Son of God, and that believing you may have life in His name" (John 20:31).

This course covers the last 13 chapters of John's Gospel.

Lessons You Will Study

Introduction to the Book 9

1. Jesus Heals a Man Born Blind (John 9) 13
2. Jesus Is the Good Shepherd (John 10) 21
3. Jesus Raises Lazarus from the Dead (John 11) 33
4. Jesus Enters Jerusalem (John 12) 45
5. Jesus Sets an Example of Humble Servanthood (John 13) . . 57
6. Jesus Is the Way, the Truth, and the Life (John 14) 67
7. Jesus Is the True Vine (John 15) 77
8. Jesus Prepares His Disciples for the Future (John 16) 85
9. Jesus Prays for His Own (John 17) 93
10. Jesus Is Arrested and Tried (John 18) 103
11. Jesus Dies for the World (John 19) 111
12. Jesus Is Raised and Appears to His Disciples (John 20–21) . . 121

Student Instructions

This Emmaus course is designed to help you know God through a better understanding of the Bible and know how it applies to your life. However, this course can never take the place of the Bible itself. The Bible is inexhaustible, and no course could give the full meaning of its truth. If studying this course is the end goal, it will become an obstacle to your growth; if it is used to inspire and equip you for your own personal study of the Bible, then it will achieve its goal. As you study the Bible using this course, prayerfully ask God to reveal His truth to you in a powerful way.

Course Sections

This course has three parts: the *lessons*, the *exams* and the *answer sheet*.

The Lessons

Each lesson is written to help explain truths from the Bible. Read each lesson through at least twice—once to get a general idea of its content, then again, slowly, looking up any Bible references given. You should always have your Bible opened to the verses or passage being studied. It is important that you read the Bible passages referenced, as some questions in the exams may be based on the Bible text.

To look up a Bible verse, keep in mind that passages in the Bible are listed by book, chapter, and verse. For instance, 2 Peter 1:21 refers to the second book of Peter, chapter 1, and verse 21. At the beginning of every Bible, there is a table of contents which lists the names of the books of the Bible and tells the page number on which each book begins. For practice, look up 2 Peter in the table of contents and turn to the page number listed; then find the chapter and verse.

The Exams

At the end of each lesson, there is an exam to assess your knowledge of the course material and the Bible passages. The exams contain multiple choice and/or True/False (T/F) questions. After you have studied a lesson, complete the exam for that lesson by recording your answers on the exam sheet that has been provided. If you have difficulty answering the questions, re-read the lesson or use the Bible as a reference.

Please note, it is best not to answer the questions based on what you *think* or have *always believed*. The questions are designed to find out if you understand the material in the course and the Bible.

What Do You Say?

In addition to the multiple choice section, each exam also contains a *What Do You Say?* question. These questions are designed for your personal reflection and to help you express your ideas and feelings as you process the lesson's content.

The Answer Sheet

Use the answer sheet provided by your group leader or instructor. When you have determined the right answer to a question on an exam, fill in the corresponding letter on the answer sheet. If you do not have someone who could provide an answer sheet, you can download one at www.emmausworldwide.org/answersheets

Submitting the Answer Sheet

When you have answered all the exam questions on the answer sheet, check them carefully. Fill in your contact information and submit your completed answer sheet to your group leader or instructor or the organization from which you received it (several options for submission are shown at next page).

OPTION 1: Send to your group leader or instructor

If you know your group leader or instructor, give them your completed answer sheet or mail it to the address listed here (if blank, go to option 2).

OPTION 2: Send to Emmaus Worldwide's head office

If no address is listed above, or if you do not know if you have a group leader or instructor and are unsure of where to send your answer sheet, choose one of the following:

MAIL the exam sheet to

Emmaus Worldwide
PO Box 1028
Dubuque, IA 52004-1028

OR

EMAIL a scan or photo

of both sides of the answer sheet
to this email address:

Exams@EmmausWorldwide.org

Receiving Your Results

You will receive back your graded exam sheet (through the same method it was submitted, either mail or email), including your final grade and a personal response from your group leader or instructor or a representative of Emmaus Worldwide.

Introduction to the Book

For the purposes of review and providing some continuity, the introduction at the beginning of chapter 1 of John Part 1 has been repeated here.

Charles R. Erdman wrote of John's gospel, "It has induced more persons to follow Christ, it has inspired more believers to loyal service, it has presented to scholars more difficult problems than any other book that could be named."

The apostle John expressed his purpose for writing his account of the life of Jesus Christ near the end of the book, in chapter 20 verse 31. Acknowledging that Jesus performed many miracles that he did *not* include in his book, John wrote:

> "But these are written that you may believe that Jesus is the Christ,the Son of God, and that believing you may have life in His name."

The seven public miracles—*signs*—that John did include "point" the reader to the fact that Jesus is God. Those miracles were:

1. Turning water into wine at the wedding in Cana of Galilee (2:9)
2. Healing the nobleman's son (4:46-54)
3. Healing the crippled man at the pool of Bethesda (5:2-9)
4. Feeding the five thousand (6:1-14)
5. Walking on the Sea of Galilee, calming the wind, and bringing the boat immediately to its destination (6:16-21)
6. Healing the man who was blind from birth (9:1-7)
7. Raising Lazarus from the dead (11:1-44)

In addition to these, John recorded an eighth sign-miracle—a post-resurrection one—which only His disciples witnessed: the miraculous catch of fish (21:1-14).

The *authorship* of this gospel has been greatly debated. This is undoubtedly because it gives such clear testimony to the deity of Jesus Christ. The attack has sought to prove that the account was not the work of an eyewitness but of an unknown genius who lived 50 to 100 years later. Thus it is supposed to reflect the church's thinking about Christ and does not comprise a record of what He Himself actually was, said, or did.

The gospel itself is anonymous as to authorship, but there are many good reasons for believing it was written by John the apostle, one of Christ's twelve disciples. For example, the author was a Jew—the style of writing, the vocabulary, the familiarity with Jewish customs and characteristics, and the background of the Old Testament reflected in this gospel all speak strongly of this. He was a Jew who lived in Palestine (1:28; 2:1, 11; 4:46; 11:18, 54; 21:1-2). He knew Jerusalem and the temple intimately (5:2; 9:7; 18:1; 19:13, 17, 20, 41; see also 2:14-16; 8:20; 10:22). He was an eyewitness of what he narrates—details of places, persons, time, manner, etc. (4:46; 5:14; 6:59; 12:21; 13:1; 14:5, 8; 18:6; 19:31). He shows intimate knowledge of the inner circle of the disciples and of Christ Himself (6:19, 60-61; 12:16; 13:22, 28; 16:19). Since the author is precise in naming other disciples yet does not name himself, it is presumed that the unnamed person of 13:23; 19:26; 20:2; 21:7, 20 is the apostle John. Three important verses for further consideration of the eyewitness character of the author are 1:14, 19:35, and 21:24.

> **The chronology of our Lord's earthly ministry is gained from this gospel.**

The *chronology* of our Lord's earthly ministry is gained from this gospel. From the other three gospels, Christ's ministry would appear to have lasted only one year. The references to the annual feasts in John supply us with the duration of approximately three years for His public ministry. Note these references: a first Feast of Passover (2:12-13); "a feast" (5:1), possibly Passover or Purim; a second Feast of Passover (6:4); the Feast of Tabernacles (7:2); the Feast of Dedication (10:22); and the last (third) Feast of Passover (12:1). John is also precise in his references to time. While the other three writers are generally content with approximate references, such as the third or ninth hours, John mentions the seventh hour (4:52), the third day (2:1), two days (11:6), and six days (12:1).

The *style and vocabulary* of this gospel are unique except for the epistles of John. The sentences are short and simple. Usually, the shorter the sentence is, the weightier the truth. The vocabulary is the most limited of all the gospels, yet the most profound in meaning. Author Leon Morris observed it is like a pool in which a child can wade and an elephant can swim. Note these important words and the number of their occurrences: Father (118), believe (100), world (78), love (45), life (37), witness, bear record, etc. (47), light (24), etc.

> **In this gospel, the Spirit of God perfects and completes the revelation of God in the person of Jesus Christ.**

One marked feature of this gospel is the occurrence of the number seven and its multiples. The ideas of perfection and completion attach to this number throughout Scripture (see Genesis 2:1-3). In this gospel, the Spirit of God perfects and completes the revelation of God in the person of Jesus Christ, so patterns based on the number seven are frequent.

The record of Jesus saying "I am ..." many times is a feature of this gospel. These are the bread of life (6:35, 41, 48, 51); the light of the world (8:12; 9:5); the door (10:7, 9); the good shepherd (10:11, 14); the resurrection and the life (11:25); the way, the truth, and the life (14:6); and the true vine (15:1, 5). Not so familiar are the seven occurrences of "I am" without a predicate (that is, the simple statement). These are found in 4:26; 6:20; 8:24, 28, 58; 13:19; and 18:5, 8. The last one is a double one.

Jesus Heals a Man Born Blind

John 9

"He went and washed and came back seeing" (9:1-12)

This incident recorded in chapter 9 may have taken place as Jesus was leaving the temple area, or it may have occurred some time after the events of chapter 8. The fact that the man had been *born* blind is drawn to our attention in verse 1 to emphasize the hopelessness of his condition and the wonder of the miracle that gave him sight.

The disciples asked a rather strange question: they wondered if the blindness had been caused by the man's own sin, or by the sin of his parents. How could the blindness have been caused by his own sin when he had been *born* blind, unless they thought God was judging him for sins He knew he would commit? They clearly thought the blindness was directly connected with sin in the family, but this was not necessarily the case. Although the presence of all sickness, suffering, and death is an ongoing result of Adam's sin (Rom. 5:12), it is not true that in any particular case a person suffers because of sins which he has committed.

Jesus told the disciples that the blindness was not a direct result of sin in the lives of either the man or his parents. God had decreed that this man, by His sovereign will, would be born blind so that the mighty works of God might be displayed. Before the man was born, God the Son knew He would give sight to those blind eyes one day. The Lord Jesus must perform a miracle of healing on him, even though it was the Sabbath day. The time of His public ministry would soon be over, and He would no longer be here on earth, performing such mighty works. This is a solemn reminder to us too that life's day is swiftly passing, and the night is coming when our service on earth will be over forever. We should use the time given to us to serve the Lord acceptably.

When Jesus was in the world as a man, He was the Light of the world in a very direct and special way (9:5). He performed miracles and taught the people. The Light of the world stood before their very eyes. Jesus is still the Light of the world, and He promised that all who come to Him will not walk in darkness (8:12). However, in this verse the Lord was speaking particularly of His public ministry on earth.

We are not told why Jesus mixed clay and spittle and put it on the blind man's eyes (9:6). Some have suggested the man had no eyeballs and that Jesus simply created them; others suggest the Lord deliberately used methods despised in the eyes of the world—He used weak and insignificant things in working out His purposes. Even today, in giving sight to the spiritually blind, God uses human beings— those who are made of the dust of the earth.

> **When a person is saved, those around him should be able to notice the difference in him.**

In verse 7, the Lord called into operation the faith of the blind man by telling him to go and wash in the pool of Siloam. No doubt he knew where the pool was and therefore was able to do as he was told. John notes that the word "Siloam" means "Sent." The One who was performing this miracle was the One who had been sent into the world by the Father. Jesus sent the blind man to wash his eyes in the pool, and after doing so he received his sight. He had never seen before at all! The miracle was instantaneous and the man was able to use his eyes immediately. What a delightful surprise it must have been for him to look for the first time upon the world in which he lived!

The Blind Man Witnesses to His Friends

The friends of the man were startled. They could hardly believe this was the same man who had begged for so long. (It should be this way also when a person is saved: those around him should be able to notice the difference in him.) Some insisted it was the same man; others were not quite so sure. But the man removed all doubt by stating that he was the one who had been born blind.

Whenever Jesus performed a miracle, it provoked all kinds of questions. Often these questions gave the believer an opportunity to witness for the

Lord. Here, people asked the man how it all happened. His testimony was simple, yet convincing. He recited the facts of his healing, giving credit to the One who had performed the miracle. At this time, the man did not realize who the Lord Jesus was. He simply referred to Him as "a Man called Jesus." But later on, the man's understanding grows and he comes to know who Jesus is. The man's questioners then wanted to know where Jesus could be found. When we witness concerning the Lord Jesus Christ, we create a desire in the hearts of others to come to know Him as well.

"One thing I know" (9:13-34)

Some of the Jewish people, probably in earnest enthusiasm over the miracle, brought the man who had been healed to the Pharisees. They may not have realized how the leaders of the Jewish people would resent what had happened, because Jesus had performed the miracle on the Sabbath day. The critical Pharisees failed to discern that God never intended the Sabbath to prevent an act of mercy or of kindness (cf. 7:23-24).

The Blind Man Witnesses to the Pharisees

In verse 15, the man had another opportunity to witness for Jesus. The Pharisees asked him how he had received his sight, and they heard the simple story once again. The man did not mention the name of Jesus here, probably not because he was afraid to do so, but because he realized now that everyone knew who had done this mighty work.

Another division arose over who Jesus was (9:16). Some of the Pharisees announced that Jesus could not be a godly man because He had broken the Sabbath. Others reasoned that a sinful man could not perform such a wonderful miracle. Jesus often caused divisions among people. People were forced to take sides and be either for Him or against Him. The Pharisees, in verse 17, asked the man who had been blind what he thought of Jesus. As yet, he did not realize that Jesus was God. But his faith had grown to the point of admitting that Jesus was a prophet. He believed that the One who had given him sight had been sent by God, and had a divine message.

Despite the testimony of the man, we read in verse 18 that many of the Jews, presumably the Pharisees, were still unwilling to believe a miracle had been performed, so they called his parents to see what they would say. Who would know better than parents if a child had been born without sight? Surely their testimony would be conclusive. The Pharisees therefore asked them whether this was their son and also how he received his sight.

The testimony of the parents was positive. This was their son, and they knew through years of heartache he had always been blind. Beyond that, they were unwilling to go. They did not know how he received his sight, they said, or who the person was who gave it. They directed the Pharisees back to their son (9:23); he could speak for himself. They had heard that any man confessing Jesus to be the Messiah would be put out of the synagogue. Excommunication was a very serious matter for any Jew. They were not willing to pay such a price, as it would mean the loss of a means of livelihood as well as a loss of all the privileges of the Jewish religion. It was for fear of the Jewish rulers, therefore, that the parents shifted the testimony back to their son.

The Pharisees Reject the Blind Man's Witness

The expression in verse 24 "Give God the glory" may have two meanings. First of all, it may be a form of oath. Perhaps the Pharisees were saying, "Now tell the truth—we know this man is a sinner." Or possibly, the Pharisees were demanding that God be given the glory for the miracle and no credit be given to Jesus, because they considered Him a sinful man. The Pharisees met with failure at every turn. Every time they tried to discredit Jesus, it resulted in bringing more honor to Him. The man's testimony was beautiful. He did not know much about Jesus, but he did know that, once he was blind, and now he could see! This was a testimony no one could deny. So it is in the case of those who have been born again. The world may doubt, scoff, and sneer, but no one can deny our testimony when we say that once we were lost, and now we have been saved by God's grace.

In verse 26 the Pharisees reopened the questioning, asking him to repeat the details. The man who had been blind was getting annoyed. He reminded them he had already told them the facts and they did not believe what he said. Why did they want to hear it again? Did they want to become disciples of Jesus? Obviously, this was asked in sarcasm! He knew very well they hated Jesus and had no desire to follow Him.

The Pharisees had failed to shake the testimony of this man, so they began to abuse him. They accused him of being a disciple of Jesus, as if that were the worst thing in the world. Then they professed to be Moses' disciples, as if that were the greatest thing possible. The Pharisees said that God had spoken to Moses and then they spoke disparagingly of Jesus. Had they believed Moses, they would have accepted the Lord Jesus. Moreover, Moses never gave sight to a man who had been born blind. One greater than Moses was in their midst, and they refused to believe it.

In verse 30, the sarcasm of the one whose eyes had been opened now became biting—something the Pharisees didn't expect. The man said in effect, "You are the teachers of the Jewish people, and yet here is a man in your midst who has the power to give sight to blind eyes and you do not know where He comes from. Shame on you!"

He was now becoming bolder in his witness. His faith was growing. He reminded them that as a general principle, God does not hear sinners or work miracles through them. God does not approve of evil people, and does not give power to them to perform mighty works. On the other hand, worshipers of God receive God's commendation and are assured of God's approval. This man realized he was the first person in all of human history to be born blind and to receive sight. He could not understand how the Pharisees could witness such a miracle and find fault with the person who performed it (9:32). If Jesus were not of God, He could never have done a miracle of this nature.

We read again in verse 34 that the Pharisees turned to abuse, insinuating that this man's blindness was the direct result of sin. What right, they thought, had *he* to teach *them*? So "they cast him out," we read in verse 34. This probably refers to more than his being cast out of the temple; no doubt it means he was excommunicated from Judaism. And yet, on what grounds? A man born blind had been given his sight on the Sabbath day. Because he would not speak evil of the One who had performed the miracle, he was excommunicated.

"Are we blind also?" (9:35-41)

Jesus now sought out this man. In effect He said to him, "If they do not want you, I will take you." Those who are cast out for Jesus' sake lose nothing. Instead, they gain a great blessing in His personal welcome and fellowship. See how Jesus led the man to personal faith in Himself as the Son of God! He simply asked the question, "Do you believe in the Son of God?" Although he had received physical sight, the man was still in need of spiritual sight. He asked the Lord who the Son of God was that he might believe in Him. In using the word "Lord" here, the man was simply saying, "Sir." The Lord Jesus now introduced Himself as the Son of God. No mere man had given him sight; no mere man had performed the impossible in his life. It was the Son of God, the One he had seen and who was now speaking with him.

At this the man simply and sweetly placed his faith in the Lord Jesus and worshiped Him (9:38). He was now a saved soul as well as a healed man. What a great day this had been in his life! He had received both physical and spiritual sight. Notice he did not worship the Lord until he knew Him to be the Son of God. Being an intelligent Jewish man, he would not worship a mere man. But as soon as he learned that the One who healed him was God, he worshiped Him—not for what He had done but for who He was.

At first glance, verse 39 seems to contradict John 3:17, "For God did not send His Son into the world to condemn the world …" But there is no real conflict. The purpose of Christ's coming into the world was not to judge but to save. However, judgment is the inevitable result for all who fail to receive Him. The preaching of the gospel has two effects. Those who admit they cannot see are given sight. But those who insist that they can see perfectly without the Lord Jesus are confirmed in their blindness.

Some of the Pharisees realized Jesus was speaking of them and of their blindness. They brazenly asked if He was insinuating that they were blind (9:40). Christ's answer may be paraphrased as follows: "If you admit yourselves to be blind and sinful and in need of a Savior, then your sins will be forgiven you. But you profess that you need nothing. You claim that you are righteous and have no sin. Therefore, there is no forgiveness of sins for you." When Jesus said, "… you would have no sin," He did not mean that they would be absolutely sinless. But comparatively speaking, they would be sinless. If they had acknowledged their blindness in failing to recognize Him as Messiah, their sin would have been as nothing compared with the sin of professing to see, yet failing to recognize Him as the Son of God.

LESSON 1 EXAM

Use the answer sheet that has been provided to complete your exam.

1. **The blind man's hopeless condition is emphasized by the fact that**
   A. he had to beg for a living.
   B. his blindness was no fault of his own.
   C. he had been born blind.
   D. he was an outcast of society.

2. **Jesus revealed to His disciples that this man's blindness**
   A. was an accident.
   B. was to be expected, as many people were born blind.
   C. was intended by God to display His power in healing him.
   D. was a good illustration of spiritual blindness.

3. **The man demonstrated _____ in following Jesus' instructions.**
   A. some medical knowledge   C. ignorance
   B. how desperate he was   D. faith in Jesus

4. **The blind man's testimony to the Pharisees caused _____ among them.**
   A. unity   C. excitement
   B. division   D. worship

5. **Why were the blind man's parents reluctant to say who had healed their son?**
   A. They knew that anyone confessing Jesus as the Messiah would be put out of the synagogue.
   B. They had not seen who had performed the miracle.
   C. They were afraid it would not be a permanent healing.
   D. They were afraid that he would no longer be able to support them by begging.

6. **The essence of the formerly blind man's testimony before the Pharisees was:**
   A. "The man called Jesus touched my eyes and now I see."
   B. "Jesus is our Messiah and He healed me."

    C. "Once I was blind, now I see."

    D. "I begged this man for money but he gave me sight instead."

7. **The argument between the formerly blind man and the Pharisees escalated when**

    A. the man sarcastically asked them if they wanted to become disciples of Jesus too.

    B. the Pharisees questioned his commitment to the law.

    C. the parents refused to authenticate their son.

    D. the disciples accused the Pharisees of abusing the man.

8. **The result of this discussion was**

    A. postponement of the inquiry.

    B. calling Jesus to testify.

    C. the formerly blind man was excommunicated.

    D. the parents were excommunicated anyway.

9. **When Jesus sought the man out later, He revealed Himself to him as the**

    A. Healer of all men.   C. Light of the world.

    B. Son of God.   D. Savior of the world.

10. **The man's response to his conversation with Jesus was to _____ Him.**

    A. fear   C. hug

    B. worship   D. run from

What Do You Say?

Cite at least one way in which Christ's healing of this man born blind parallels the process of salvation.

LESSON 2

Jesus Is the Good Shepherd

John 10

"I am the door of the sheep" (10:1-10)

In the Old Testament, there are numerous references to the relationship between God and Israel as being like that of a shepherd and his sheep (e.g. Ps. 80:1 & Ezek. 34:10-16). In addition, God called Israel's leaders "wicked shepherds" of His people (e.g. Jer. 23:1-4 & Zechariah 11). The Pharisees claimed to be the current-day rightful shepherds of the people of Israel. It was to them, in particular, that Jesus now spoke.

Jesus described the Jewish nation as a "sheepfold." A sheepfold was an enclosure in which sheep were sheltered at night and which had one opening into it. Jesus Christ entered the nation of Israel the "authorized" way, as it were, being God's appointed Messiah and having fulfilled prophecy. These Pharisees had not come in the right way; they had, as it were, climbed over the wall. They were not true shepherds; in effect, they were thieves and robbers. They sought to rule over Israel for personal gain and did everything to hinder the people from accepting God's appointed Messiah.

The Sheep Respond to Their Shepherd

There is considerable disagreement as to the identity of the doorkeeper (10:3). Some think this expression refers to the prophets of the Old Testament who foretold the coming of the Christ. Others believe it refers to John the Baptist, since he was the forerunner of the true Shepherd.

Others think the doorkeeper is the Holy Spirit who opens the door for the entrance of the Lord into hearts and lives.

The sheep heard the shepherd's voice. They recognized his voice as that of the true shepherd. Just as literal sheep recognize the voice of their own shepherd, so there were those among the Jewish people who recognized their Messiah. Throughout John's gospel, we have heard the Shepherd calling His own sheep by name. He called to several disciples in chapter 1, and they all heard His voice and responded. And as recently as chapter 9, He took the initiative and called the blind man, an individual person. The Lord Jesus still calls those who will receive Him as Savior, and the call is personal and individual. The expression "and leads them out" may refer to the fact that the Lord led those who heard His voice out of the sheepfold of Israel. There, they were shut up and enclosed; they experienced no liberty under the Law. Christ leads His sheep into the freedom of His grace. Referring to the blind beggar healed just previously, Warren Wiersbe comments, "The Pharisees *threw* the beggar out of the synagogue, but Jesus *led* him out of Judaism and into the flock of God!" The Pharisees had been assisting the work of the Lord without knowing it!

When the true Shepherd puts forth His sheep, He does not drive them, He leads them (10:4). He is ever out in front of the sheep, their Savior, their Guide, and their Example. Those who are genuinely His sheep follow Him. They do not *become* sheep by following His example—they become sheep by believing in Him—but once they belong to Him, they have a desire to go where He leads. The same instinct that enables a sheep to recognize the voice of the true Shepherd also prompts it to flee from a stranger. The strangers were the Pharisees and other leaders of the Jewish people who were only interested in the sheep for their own personal advantage. The man who received his sight illustrates this. He recognized the voice of Christ but knew that the Pharisees were strangers. He therefore refused to obey them, even though it meant being excommunicated. It is distinctly stated now that Jesus spoke these words to the Pharisees, but they did not understand—the reason being they were not true sheep. If they had been, they would have heard His voice and would have followed Him.

> Christianity is not a creed, or a church. It is a person, and that person is the Lord Jesus Christ.

In verse 7 Jesus uses a new illustration: He Himself is the Door of the sheep. It is no longer a question of entering into the sheepfold of Israel. Now the elect sheep of Israel pass out of Judaism and come to Christ, the Door.

We are told in verse 8 that others had come before Christ, claiming authority and position. But the elect sheep of Israel did not hear them because they knew they were claiming what did not rightfully belong to them.

Jesus Is the Door to Salvation

Verse 9 is simple enough for a child to understand, yet it can never be exhausted by even the most learned scholar. Christ is the Door. Christianity is not a creed or a church—it is a Person, and that Person is the Lord Jesus Christ. "If anyone enters by Me, he will be saved." Salvation can only be received through Christ. Baptism will not do; neither will the Lord's Supper. We must enter in by Christ alone. The invitation is for any person. Christ is the Savior of Jew and Gentile alike. But to be saved, a man must enter in. He must receive Christ by faith. It is a personal act, and without it there is no salvation. Those who do enter in are saved from the penalty and power of sin, and eventually from its very presence. After they put their trust in Him for salvation, they go "in and out." That is, they go into the presence of God by faith to worship, and then they go out into the world to witness for the Lord. It is a picture of perfect liberty in the service of the Lord. Those who enter find *pasture*; Christ is not only the Savior and the One who gives freedom, He is also the Sustainer. His sheep find sustaining nourishment in the written Word of God.

> The more we yield to the control of the Holy Spirit, the more we enjoy the life which has been given to us.

A contrast is presented in verse 10. The thief steals, kills, and destroys. But the Lord Jesus does not come to the human heart for any selfish reason. He comes to give. He comes that men and women, boys and girls, "may have life, and that they may have it more abundantly." We receive life the moment we receive Him as our Savior. After we are saved there are degrees of enjoyment. The more we yield to the control of the Holy Spirit, the more we enjoy the life which has been given to us. We not only have life, we have it more abundantly.

"I am the good Shepherd" (10:11-18)

Many times the Lord Jesus used the expression "I am," one of the titles of deity. Each time, He was making a claim to equality with God. Here He presented Himself as the Good Shepherd, the One who would lay down His life for the sheep. Ordinarily, the sheep were slain for the shepherd. But

Christ Jesus died for the flock. In contrast (10:12) we read of a hireling—one who was paid for his services. The Pharisees were hirelings. Their interest in the people was prompted by the money they received in return. The hireling did not own the sheep. When danger came, he ran away and left the sheep to the mercy of predators. We do what we do because we are what we are. The hireling was more interested in his own welfare than in their good. There are hirelings in the church today—men who choose the ministry as a comfortable occupation, without true love for God's sheep.

In verse 14 the Lord speaks of Himself as the Good Shepherd. "Good" here means "worthy, choice, excellent." He is all of these. Then He speaks of the intimate relationship that exists between Himself and His sheep. He knows His own, and His own know Him. This is a very wonderful truth.

> **Ordinarily, the sheep were slain for the shepherd. But Christ Jesus died for the flock.**

In verse 15 the Lord compared His relationship to the sheep with the relationship that existed between Himself and His Father. The same union, communion, intimacy, and knowledge that there is between the Father and the Son exists between the Shepherd and the sheep. "And I lay down My life for the sheep," He said. Again we have one of the many statements of the Lord Jesus in which He anticipated His death on the cross as a Substitute for sinners.

Jesus Speaks of the Salvation of the Gentiles

Verse 16 is the key to the entire chapter. The "other sheep" to whom the Lord referred here were the Gentiles. His coming was especially in connection with the sheep of Israel, but He also had in mind the salvation of Gentiles. The Gentile sheep were not of the Jewish fold. But the great heart of Jesus went out to these sheep as well, and He was under divine compulsion to bring them to Himself. He knew they would be more ready than the Jewish people to hear His voice. Notice His use of the word "flock," not "fold." There was a change from the *fold of Judaism* to the *flock of Christianity*. This verse gives a preview of the fact that in Christ, Jew and Gentile would be made one, and that the former distinctions between these peoples would disappear.

In verses 17 and 18 Christ explained what He would do to bring both Jews and Gentiles to Himself: He would die and then rise again. He spoke of laying down His life and taking it again by His own power. He could only do this because He is God. The Father loved the Son for His willingness to die and rise again in order that lost sheep might be saved. No one could take the Lord's life from Him. He is God, and thus was greater than all the murderous plots of His creatures. He had power in Himself to lay down His life, and He also had power to take it again. But men killed the Lord Jesus, didn't they? They did. This is clearly stated in Acts 2:23 and in 1 Thessalonians 2:15. He allowed them to do it, and this was an exhibition of His power to lay down His life. Furthermore, He "gave up His spirit" (19:30) as an act of His own strength and will. "This command I have received from My Father," He said. The Father had instructed Him to lay down His life and to rise again from among the dead. His death and resurrection were an essential part of the Father's will.

"He has a demon" (10:19-21)

Again the Lord Jesus caused a division among the Jews. His entrance into the world, homes, and hearts produces a sword rather than peace (Matt. 10:34). Only when people receive Him as Lord and Savior do they know the peace of God. The Lord Jesus Christ was the only perfect man who ever lived. He never said a wrong word or committed an evil deed. Yet such is the depravity of man that when He came, speaking words of love and wisdom, men said He had a demon and was mad, and should be ignored. But some thought otherwise. They recognized His words and works as those of a good person and not of a demon.

"My sheep ... shall never perish" (10:22-30)

At this point, there is a break in the narrative. Jesus was no longer speaking to the Pharisees but to the Jews in general. We do not know what time elapsed between verse 21 and verse 22. Incidentally, this is the only mention in the Bible of the Feast of Dedication. It is generally believed that this feast was instituted by Judas Maccabeus when the temple was rededicated after being defiled by Antiochus Epiphanes in 165 BC. It was an annual feast, instituted by the Jewish people, and not one of the feasts of Jehovah. It was winter—both, actually and spiritually. The public ministry of the Lord Jesus was almost over, and He was about to demonstrate His complete dedication to God the Father by His death on the cross.

Verse 24 records a question asked of Jesus. Solomon's porch mentioned here was a covered area, adjoining Herod's temple. As the Lord walked there, there would have been plenty of room for the Jews to gather around Him. "How long do You keep us in doubt?" they asked Him. "If You are the Christ, tell us plainly."

In verse 25 Jesus again reminded them of His words and His works. He had often told them that He was the Messiah, and His miracles proved His claim to be true. Again He reminded the Jews that He performed His miracles by authority of His Father and for His Father's glory. In doing so, He showed He was indeed the One the Father had sent into the world. But their unwillingness to receive Him proved they were not His sheep. If they had been set apart to belong to Him, they would have shown a willingness to believe Him.

Jesus Speaks of the Eternal Security of the Believer

Starting in verse 27, Jesus teaches in unmistakable terms that no true sheep of His will ever perish. The eternal security of the believer is a glorious fact. Those who are true sheep of Christ hear His voice. They hear it when the gospel is preached, and they respond by believing in Him. Thereafter, they hear His voice day by day and obey His word. The Lord Jesus knows His sheep. He knows each one by name. Not one will escape His attention. Not one will be lost through an oversight or carelessness on His part. Christ's sheep follow Him. They recognize the true Shepherd and stay close to Him.

Christ gives eternal life to His sheep (10:28). This means life that will last forever. It is not life that is conditional on their behavior. It is eternal (everlasting) life. But *eternal* life is also a quality of life. It is the life of the Lord Jesus Himself—a life capable of enjoying the things of God down here, and suitable to heaven itself. Note these next words carefully: *"They shall never perish."* If any sheep of Christ ever perished, then the Lord Jesus would fail to keep a promise, and this is not possible. Jesus Christ is God, and He cannot fail. He has promised that no sheep of His will ever spend eternity in hell.

Does this mean then that a person may put their trust in Christ and then live any way he pleases? Can he be saved and then carry on in the sinful pleasures of this world? *No!* If he is genuinely one of Christ's sheep, he no longer desires to do these things. He wants to follow the Shepherd. We do not live a Christian life in order to become a Christian or in order to retain our salvation. We live a Christian life because we are Christians. We desire to live a holy life not out of fear of losing our salvation, but out of gratitude to the One who died for us. The doctrine of eternal security does not encourage careless living; rather, it is a strong motive for holy living.

No one is able to snatch a believer out of Christ's hand. His hand is almighty. It created the world; it even now sustains the world. There is no power that can snatch a sheep from His grasp. Not only is the believer in the hand of Christ, he is in the Father's hand as well. This is a twofold guarantee of safety. God the Father is greater than all, and no one can snatch a believer out of the Father's hand.

In verse 30, the Lord added a further claim to equality with God. "I and My Father are one." Here the thought probably is that Christ and the Father are one in power. Jesus had been speaking about the power that protects the sheep. He added the explanation that His power is the same as the power of God the Father. Of course, the same is true of all the other attributes of deity. The Lord Jesus Christ is God in the fullest sense and is equal with the Father in every way.

> **The doctrine of eternal security does not encourage careless living; rather, it is a strong motive for holy living.**

"The Jews took up stones ... to stone Him" (10:31-39)

We see from verse 31 that there was no question in the minds of the Jews as to what Christ meant. He was setting forth His deity, so they took up stones to kill Him.

Before they had a chance to hurl the stones, He reminded them of the many miracles He had performed by commandment from His Father. Which of these good works had so infuriated them that they wanted to kill Him? The Jews stated plainly that they sought to slay Him because He had spoken blasphemy by claiming to be equal with God. They refused to admit He was anything more than a man, yet He made Himself God as far as His claims were concerned. They would not tolerate this.

Jesus Uses the Old Testament to Prove His Argument

In verse 34 Jesus quoted to the Jews from Psalm 82:6. He called this a part of their Law. In other words, it was taken from the Old Testament Scriptures which they acknowledged to be the inspired Word of God. The complete verse is as follows: "I said, 'You are gods, and all of you are children of the Most High.'" The psalm was addressed to the judges of Israel. They were called "gods" not because they were actually divine, but because they represented God when they judged the people. The Hebrew word for "gods" and "judges" is the same. It could also be translated "mighty ones." (It is clear from the rest of the psalm that they were only men and not deities in that they judged unjustly, showed respect of persons, and otherwise perverted justice.) Jesus used this Scripture to show that God used the word "gods" to describe men to whom the word of God came. In other words, these men were spokesmen for God; Jehovah spoke to the nation of Israel through them. "And the Scripture cannot be broken," said Jesus, testifying to the divine inspiration of the Old Testament. To Him they were infallible writings which must be fulfilled and which could not be denied. In fact, the very words of Scripture are inspired, not just its thoughts or ideas—His whole argument is based on the single word "gods."

Jesus was using the literary technique of arguing from the lesser to the greater in verse 36: If unjust judges were called "gods" in the Old Testament, how much more right had He to say He was the Son of God! The word of God *came* to them; He *was* and *is* the Word of God incarnate. They were *called* gods; He *was* and *is* God. It could never have been said of them that the Father had sanctified them and sent them into the world. They were born into the world like all other sons of fallen Adam. But Jesus was sanctified (set apart) by God the Father from all eternity to be the Savior of the world, and He was sent into the world from heaven where He had always dwelt with His Father. Thus Jesus had

> **The word of God came to them; Jesus was and is the Word of God incarnate.**

every right to claim equality with God. He was not blaspheming when He claimed to be the Son of God, equal with the Father. The Jews themselves used the term "gods" to apply to corrupt men who were mere spokesmen or judges for God—how much more could He claim the title because He actually *was* and *is* God.

In verse 37, Jesus appealed to the miracles which He performed as proof of His divine commission. However, note the expression "the works of My Father." Miracles, in themselves, are not a proof of deity. We read in the Bible of evil beings having the power at times to perform miracles. But Christ's miracles were the works of His Father. They proved Him to be the Messiah in a twofold way: they were the miracles which the Old Testament Scriptures predicted would be performed by the Messiah, and they were miracles of mercy and compassion, works that benefited mankind and which would not be performed by an evil person.

Verse 38 has been helpfully paraphrased as follows: "If I do the works of My Father, then, though you may not be convinced by what I say, be convinced by what I do. Though you resist the evidence of My words, yield to the evidence of My works. In this way, learn to know and believe that I and My Father are indeed one, He in me and I in Him, and that in claiming to be His Son, I speak no blasphemy." Again the Jews realized that instead of denying His previous claims, Jesus had only strengthened them. Therefore, they made another attempt to arrest Him, but He eluded them once more. The time was not far distant now when He would permit Himself to be taken by them—but as yet, His hour had not come.

"The things that John spoke about this Man were true" (10:40-42)

The Lord went now to the very place beyond the Jordan where He had begun His public ministry (10:40). His three years of wondrous words and mighty works were drawing to a close. He ended them where He began them—outside the established order of Judaism, in a place of rejection and loneliness. Many now came to Him, and those who came were probably sincere believers. They were willing to bear His reproach, to take their place with Him outside the camp of Israel (cf. Heb. 13:13). These followers paid a glowing tribute to John the Baptist. They remembered that John's ministry was not spectacular or sensational, but it was true. Everything he said about Jesus was fulfilled in His ministry. This should encourage each one who is a Christian. We may not be able to do mighty miracles or gain public attention, but at least we can bear a true testimony to our Lord and Savior. This is of great value in God's sight.

It is lovely to notice that in spite of His rejection by the nation of Israel, the Lord Jesus did find some humble and receptive hearts. "Many," we are told, "believed on Him there." Thus it is in every age. There is always a remnant of the people who are willing to take their place with the Lord Jesus, cast out by the world, hated and scorned, but enjoying the sweet fellowship of the Son of God.

LESSON 2 EXAM

Use the answer sheet that has been provided to complete your exam.

1. **Jesus' teaching in chapter 9 is a continuation of His verbal exchange with**
    A. His disciples.
    C. the blind man He had healed.
    B. the Pharisees.
    D. the Jews in the synagogue.

2. **In His analogy, Jesus described the _____ as a sheepfold.**
    A. Jewish nation
    C. Romans
    B. Gentiles
    D. Pharisees

3. **As the Shepherd, Jesus calls His sheep**
    A. as part of a large group.
    B. as a random sample from a larger group.
    C. as the total of a small group.
    D. individually, by name.

4. **How is Jesus the Door?**
    A. He is the only way to salvation.
    B. He is the One who will let us into heaven.
    C. He shuts out those who disobey Him.
    D. We have to knock and ask to be saved.

5. **The concept of "going in and out" is described by the course author as**
    A. being sustained spiritually by the Word of God.
    B. worshiping the Lord in private and witnessing for Him in public.
    C. perfect liberty in the service of the Lord.
    D. all the above.

6. **Jesus presented Himself as the good Shepherd who**
    A. would take the sheep to comfortable pasture.
    B. would lay down His life for the sheep.
    C. would find the sheep when they got lost.
    D. would not leave the sheep alone in the wilderness.

7. **The "other sheep" to which Jesus referred are understood to be**
   A. some righteous Israelites.   C. the Gentiles.
   B. Old Testament Jews.   D. Sadducees.

8. **The Lord Jesus taught that those who put their trust in Him to save them**
   A. can lose their salvation under certain conditions.
   B. will have to wait until they die before knowing if they are fit for heaven.
   C. will have to do certain things to guarantee their salvation.
   D. can never perish.

9. **"The doctrine of eternal security does not encourage _____; rather, it is a strong motive for _____."**
   A. apathy towards the Lord / love for the Lord
   B. holy living / careless living
   C. careless living / holy living
   D. keeping God's commandments / ignoring God's commandments

10. **The Jews again tried to stone Jesus to death because**
    A. He had healed the blind man on a Sabbath.
    B. He persisted in claiming equality with God.
    C. He was, in their view, profaning Scripture.
    D. He challenged their authority over the people.

What Do You Say?

Comment from your own experience on the "quality" of the eternal life that Christ gives the believer.

EXAM 2

Jesus Raises Lazarus from the Dead

John 11

"This sickness is not unto death" (11:1-4)

We now come to the last miracle in the *public* ministry of the Lord Jesus as recorded by John. In some senses, it was the greatest of all—the raising of a dead man. Lazarus lived in the little village of Bethany, about two miles east of Jerusalem, with his sisters Mary and Martha. John explains in verse 2 that it was Mary of Bethany who had anointed the Lord Jesus with ointment and wiped His feet with her hair. This remarkable act of devotion was emphasized by the Holy Spirit. The Lord loves the willing affection of His people.

Jesus was apparently still on the east side of the Jordan River when Lazarus took sick. The sisters immediately sent Him word, and they appealed to His love for their brother as a special reason why He should come and help.

"This sickness is not unto death," Jesus said. He did not mean that Lazarus would not die, but that death would not be the final outcome of this sickness. The real purpose of the sickness was "the glory of God, that the Son of God may be glorified through it." God allowed this to happen so Jesus would come and raise Lazarus from the dead and thus be manifested again as the true Messiah. Men would glorify God for this mighty miracle.

There is no suggestion that Lazarus's sickness was a result of some particular sin in his life. On the contrary, he is presented as a devoted disciple and a special object of Christ's love.

"He stayed two more days" (11:5-16)

When sickness enters our homes, we are not to conclude that God is displeased with us. Here, sickness was directly linked with His love. We would naturally think that if the Lord really loved these three believers, then He would hurry to their home. Instead, when He heard the news, He remained two days where He was. God's delays are not God's denials. If our prayers are not answered immediately, perhaps He is teaching us to wait, and if we wait patiently, we will find that He will answer our prayers in a much more marvelous way than we anticipated. Not even the Lord's love for Martha and Mary and Lazarus could force Him to act ahead of the proper time. Everything He did was in obedience to His Father's will and in keeping with the divine plan. Then, after two seemingly wasted days, Jesus proposed to the disciples that they should all go into Judea once more.

The disciples were still painfully aware of how the Jews had sought to kill Christ after He had given sight to the blind man (11:8). How could He even think of going into Judea in the face of such personal danger? The Lord's response is instructive. There are twelve hours of light in a day in which to work. As long as a man works during this allotted time, there is no danger of his stumbling or falling as he can see where he's going and what he's doing. The light keeps him from accidental death through stumbling. The spiritual meaning is that because Jesus was walking in obedience to God's will, there was no danger that He'd be killed before the appointed time. He would be preserved until His work was done. In a sense, this is a principle that is true of every believer. If we are walking in fellowship with the Lord and doing His will, no power on earth can kill us before God's time. In contrast, the man who walks in the night is one who is not faithful to God, but living in self-will. This man stumbles easily because he does not have divine guidance to illuminate his way.

> God's delays are not God's denials. If our prayers are not answered immediately, perhaps He is teaching us to wait.

Jesus Speaks of Death as Sleep

In verse 11 Jesus spoke of Lazarus's death as sleep. In the New Testament, sleep is *never* applied to the soul, only to the body; the believer's *soul* goes to be with Christ, which is far better (Phil. 1:23). The Lord Jesus revealed His omniscience in this statement. He knew Lazarus was already dead, although the only report He had been given was that Lazarus was sick. He knew because He is God. He was going to awaken Lazarus. While any man may awaken another out of physical sleep, only the Lord could awaken Lazarus out of death. Jesus expressed here His intention of doing that very thing.

The disciples did not understand Christ's reference to sleep. In verse 12 they said in effect, "If Lazarus is sleeping, he'll recover." Perhaps they believed sleeping to be a symptom of recovery and concluded that if Lazarus was able to sleep soundly, then he had passed the crisis and would get well. The verse might also mean that if physical sleep were the only thing wrong with Lazarus, then there was no need to go to Bethany to help him. Perhaps the disciples were fearful for their own safety and seized upon this excuse for not going to Bethany. But Jesus was referring to death when He spoke of sleep, and He now spoke plainly—Lazarus was dead. It is interesting that the disciples received the news calmly. They did not ask the Lord, "How do You know?" He spoke with complete authority, and they did not question His knowledge.

Jesus was not glad that Lazarus had died, but in verse 15 we read that He was glad He was not at Bethany at the time. Had He been there, Lazarus would not have died. The disciples would see a greater miracle than the prevention of death—they would see a man raised from the dead. In this way, their faith would be strengthened. Therefore, the Lord said He was glad for their sakes that He had not been at Bethany. "… that you may believe," He added. The miracle they were about to see would greatly strengthen their faith in Him. He urged them, therefore, to go with Him.

Verse 16 gives us insight into the disciple Thomas. He reasoned that if Jesus went to Bethany, the Jews would kill Him. So if the disciples went with Jesus, they too would be killed. In a spirit of pessimism and gloom, he urged them all to go with Jesus. His words are not an example of great faith or courage, but of discouragement.

"I am the resurrection and the life" (11:17-27)

The fact that Lazarus had been in the grave for four days was added as proof that he was dead. Notice how the Holy Spirit safeguards the fact that the resurrection of Lazarus *was* a miracle.

Bethany's proximity to Jerusalem made it possible for many of the Jews to visit Mary and Martha, and to comfort them. Little did they realize that in a short time their comfort would no longer be needed! This house of mourning would be turned into a house of rejoicing.

As soon as Martha heard that Jesus was approaching, she ran out to meet Him (11:20). The meeting took place just outside the village. We are not told why Mary remained home. Perhaps she had not received the report of Jesus' arrival. Maybe she was paralyzed by grief. Or was she simply waiting in a spirit of prayer and trust? Did she sense what was about to happen because of her closeness to the Lord? We do not know.

> **All things are in God's hands, and nothing happens to one of His own without His permission.**

It had been real faith that had enabled Martha to believe that Jesus could have prevented Lazarus from dying (11:21). Still, her faith was imperfect. She thought He could only do this if He were physically present. She did not realize He could heal from a distance, still less that He could raise the dead. Often, in times of sorrow, we talk like Martha. We think that if such and such a drug or medicine had been discovered, then this loved one would not have died. But all these things are in God's hands, and nothing happens to one of His own without His permission. Again, Martha's faith shone out. She did not know *how* Jesus would help, but she believed He would. She had confidence that God would grant Him His request and that He would bring good out of this seeming tragedy. But she did not dare to believe her brother would be raised from the dead. The word Martha used for "ask" is the word normally used to describe a creature supplicating the Creator. Obviously Martha did not recognize the deity of the Lord Jesus. She realized that He was a great and unusual Man, but probably no greater than the prophets of old.

Jesus Speaks to Martha about Resurrection

To lift her faith to greater heights, Jesus made the startling announcement that Lazarus would rise again. He dealt tenderly with this sorrowing woman to lead her step by step to faith in Him as the Son of

God. Martha knew her brother would rise from the dead some day, but she had no thought that it could happen right then and there. She believed in the resurrection of the dead and that it would happen in what she called "the last day." In reply the Lord said in effect, "You do not understand Me, Martha. I do not mean that Lazarus will rise again at the last day. I am God, and I have the power of resurrection and of life. I can and will raise Lazarus from the dead right now."

Then the Lord looked forward to the time when all believers will be raised, the time when He comes back to take His people home (11:25). At that time, there will be two "classes" of believers. There will be those who have died in faith, and those who are still alive at His return. He comes to the first as the *resurrection* and to the second as the *life*. The first are described in the latter part of verse 25—"He who believes in Me, though he may be dead, he shall live." Those believers who have died before Christ's coming will be raised from the dead. The second class is described in verse 26. Those believers who are alive at the time of the Savior's coming will never die. They will be changed in a moment, in the twinkling of an eye (1 Cor. 15:52), and taken home to heaven with those who have been raised from the dead. What precious truths have been revealed to us as a result of Lazarus's death! God brings sweetness out of bitterness and gives beauty for ashes. Then the Lord pointedly asked Martha, to test her faith, "Do you believe this?" Martha's faith blazed

> God brings sweetness out of bitterness and gives beauty for ashes.

out in noontime splendor. She confessed Jesus to be the Christ, the Son of God, whom the prophets had predicted would come into the world. And notice, she made this confession *before* Jesus raised her brother out from among the dead!

"Jesus wept" (11:28-37)

Immediately after this confession, Martha rushed back to the village and greeted Mary with the breathless announcement, "The Teacher has come and is calling for you." The Creator of the universe and the Savior of the world had come to Bethany and was calling for Mary. It is still the same today. This same wonderful Person stands and calls people to Himself in the words of the gospel. Each one is invited to respond by receiving Him into their heart and life. Mary's response was immediate. She rose quickly and went to Jesus (11:29).

Now Jesus met Martha and Mary outside the village of Bethany. The Jews did not know He was near since Martha's announcement of the fact to Mary had been a secret one. Not unnaturally, they concluded that Mary had gone out to the grave to weep there.

Mary fell down at Christ's feet. It may have been an act of worship, or simply that she was overcome with grief. Like Martha, she uttered the regret that Jesus had not been present in Bethany, for in that case, Lazarus would not have died. To see Mary and her friends in sorrow caused Jesus to groan and to be troubled. Undoubtedly, He thought of all the sadness, suffering, and death which had come into the world as a result of man's sin. This caused Him inward grief. The Greek word here is a strong term. He asked where Lazarus was buried. He knew, of course, but asked the question to awaken expectation, to encourage faith and to call forth man's cooperation.

Verse 35 is the shortest in the English Bible. It records one of three instances where the Lord is said to have wept. (He wept also in sorrow over the city of Jerusalem and in the garden of Gethsemane.) His weeping was evidence of His true humanity. He shed tears of grief when He witnessed the effects of sin on the human race. It is not improper for Christians to weep when their loved ones are taken. However, Christians do not sorrow as others who have no hope (1 Thess. 4:13).

The Jews saw in the tears of Jesus proof of His love for Lazarus. But He also loved *them* just as much, though many of them failed to understand this. Some recognized Him as the same One who had given sight to the blind man. Why, they wondered, had He not prevented Lazarus from dying? Of course, He could have done so, but instead He was going to perform a mightier miracle.

"Lazarus, come forth!" (11:38-44)

The Lord was filled with inward heaviness. It would seem that the grave was a cave under the earth, into which one would have to descend by a ladder or a flight of stairs. A stone was placed on top of the cave. Verse 39 records that Jesus commanded the onlookers to remove the stone from the grave. He could have done this Himself by merely speaking the word. However, God does not ordinarily do for men what they can do for themselves. Martha expressed horror at the thought of opening the grave. Her brother's body had been there for four days and had begun to decompose! Apparently, they had not embalmed the body; Lazarus would have been buried the same day he died, as was the custom. The fact that Lazarus was in the grave for four days is important. He was certainly not asleep or in a coma. His resurrection can only be explained as a miracle.

It is not clear when Christ had spoken the words of verse 40. In verse 23, He had told Martha that her brother would rise again. What He said here was presumably the substance of what He had previously told her. Notice the order in this verse. "Believe … see." It is as if the Lord Jesus had said, "If you will just believe, you will see Me perform a miracle that only God could perform. You will see the glory of God revealed in Me. But first you must believe, and then you will see."

In verse 41, the stone was then removed from the grave. Before performing the miracle, Jesus thanked His Father for having heard His prayer. No previous prayer of the Lord Jesus is recorded in this chapter; no doubt He had been speaking to His Father continually during this entire period and had prayed that God's name might be glorified in the resurrection of Lazarus. Here He thanked the Father in anticipation of the event. He prayed audibly in order that the people might understand that the Father had sent Him, that the Father told Him what to do and what to say, and that He always acted in dependence upon God. Here again the essential union of God the Father and the Lord Jesus Christ is emphasized.

> **First you must believe, and then you will see.**

Verse 43 records one of the few instances in the New Testament where Jesus is said to have cried with a loud voice. It has been suggested that if He had not mentioned Lazarus by name, then all the dead in the graves would have risen! How did Lazarus come forth? We really don't know—maybe he hobbled out, maybe he crawled out on hands and knees; maybe the fact that his body was wrapped tightly in grave clothes made it impossible for him to have come out by his own power. The fact that his face was bound about with a cloth is further proof that he had been dead; no one could have lived for four days with his face bound like that. The Lord commanded the people to loose Lazarus and to let him go.

"From that day on, they plotted to put Him to death" (11:45-57)

To many of the onlookers, this miracle unmistakably proclaimed the deity of the Lord Jesus Christ, and they believed in Him. Who else but God could call forth a dead body from the grave? But the effect of a miracle on a person's life depends on his moral condition. If a man's heart is evil, rebellious, and hardened, he will not believe even if he saw a dead person raised from the grave. That was the case we see in verse 46 (read Luke 16:31 for Christ's concluding statement after telling about *another* Lazarus). Some of the unbelieving Jews who witnessed the miracle went to the Pharisees to report what had happened in Bethany. Why? Probably so that the Pharisees might be further stirred up against Christ and seek to put Him to death.

> **If a man's heart is evil, rebellious, and hardened, he will not believe even if he saw a dead person raised from the grave.**

The chief priests and Pharisees gathered together to discuss what action should be taken. "What are we going to do about this?" they said. "Why are we so slow to take some action? This man is performing many miracles, and we are doing nothing to stop him." The Jewish leaders spoke these words to their own condemnation. It has been well said,

> "This is a marvelous admission. Even our Lord's worst enemies confess that our Lord did miracles, and many miracles. Can we doubt that they would have denied the truth of His miracles if they could? But they do not seem to have attempted it. They were too many, too public, and too thoroughly witnessed for them to dare to deny them. How, in the face of this fact, modern infidels and skeptics can talk of our Lord's miracles as being impostures and delusions, they would do well to explain! If the Pharisees who lived in our Lord's time, and who moved heaven and earth to oppose His progress, never dared to dispute the fact that He worked miracles, it is absurd to begin denying His miracles now, after [twenty] centuries have passed away."

In verse 48 we see that the Jews felt they could no longer remain inactive. If they did not intervene, the mass of the people would be persuaded by the miracles of Jesus. If the people acknowledged Jesus as their King, it would mean trouble with Rome. The Romans would think that Jesus had come to overthrow their empire; they would move in and punish the Jews. The expression "take away both our place and nation" means that the Romans would destroy the temple and scatter the Jewish people. These very things took place in AD 70—not, however, because the Jews accepted the Lord, but because they rejected Him.

Caiaphas Prophesies about Jesus' Death

Caiaphas was high priest from AD 26 to 36. He presided at the religious trial of Christ and was present when Peter and John were brought before the Sanhedrin (Acts 4:6). He was not a believer in Christ, in spite of what he said here. The chief priests and Pharisees, he argued, were wrong in thinking the Jews would die on account of Jesus. On the contrary, Jesus would die for the Jewish nation (11:50). It was expedient (better) that Jesus should die for the people, so that the whole nation would not perish. Why, it sounds as if Caiaphas really understood the reason for Jesus' coming into the world! We would almost think he had accepted Jesus as the Substitute for sinners! But no! What he said was true, but he himself did not believe in Jesus to the saving of his soul.

He did not speak "of himself," that is, he did not make up these things by himself. He did not speak this of his own will. The message he uttered was given him by God. It was a prophecy that Jesus would die for the nation of Israel. It was given to Caiaphas because he was high priest that year. God spoke through him because of the office he held, and not because of his own personal righteousness, for he was a sinful man. The prophecy of Caiaphas was not only that Jesus would die for Israel; He would also gather together His elect among the Gentiles of the earth. Some think Caiaphas was referring to Jewish people scattered abroad throughout the earth, but more probably he was unwittingly referring to Gentiles who would believe on Christ through the preaching of the gospel.

The Pharisees were not convinced by the miracle at Bethany—in fact, they were more hostile than ever. In verse 53, we read that from then onwards, they plotted His death with new intensity. Aware of the mounting hostility of the Jews, Jesus retreated to a city called Ephraim. We do not know where Ephraim was except that it was in a quiet, secluded area near the wilderness.

The announcement that the Jews' Passover was at hand reminds us we are coming to the close of the Lord's public ministry (11:55). It was at this very Passover that He was to be crucified. Prior to the Passover, the people were required to go to Jerusalem to purify themselves. For instance, if a Jewish person had touched a dead body, he must go through a certain ritual to be cleansed from his ceremonial defilement. This purifying was done through various types of washings and offerings. The Jewish people were thus seeking to purify themselves, while at the same time they were planning the death of the Passover Lamb. What a terrible exposure of the wickedness of the heart of man!

As the people gathered in Jerusalem, they began to think about the miracle worker named Jesus. Would He come to the feast? The question "What do you think—that He will not come to the feast?" might better be broken down this way: "What do you think? Surely he will not come to the feast." They knew official orders had gone out from the chief priests and the Pharisees for Jesus to be arrested. Any Jewish person who knew of His whereabouts was commanded to notify the authorities so that He might be taken and put to death.

LESSON 3 EXAM

Use the answer sheet that has been provided to complete your exam.

1. **When Jesus said that Lazarus's sickness was not unto death, He meant that**
   A. Lazarus would never die.
   B. death would not be the final outcome of this sickness.
   C. He would go and heal Lazarus.
   D. Lazarus would recover from this sickness.

2. **The reason for Lazarus's sickness was**
   A. that God would be glorified.
   B. because he had a major sin in his life.
   C. because God was displeased with him.
   D. that his sisters would understand the purpose of sorrow.

3. **Why was Jesus not afraid to go back to Judea?**
   A. He knew His disciples would protect Him.
   B. He was walking in obedience to God's will.
   C. He wanted to be with Mary and Martha in their sorrow.
   D. He was sure the Jews would not find out He was there.

4. **In the New Testament, "sleep" often refers to**
   A. apathy.
   B. the state of the soul at death.
   C. the separation of soul and spirit at death.
   D. the state of the body at death.

5. **Jesus' conversation with Martha was designed to**
   A. explain the reason for His delay in coming.
   B. assure her of His love.
   C. lift her faith to greater heights.
   D. express His sorrow about her loss.

6. **In verse 25, Jesus looks forward to the time when**
   A. He will raise Lazarus.
   B. all believers who have died will be raised.
   C. He will rule on earth.
   D. the earth will be destroyed.

EXAM 3

7. **In verse 26, Jesus was referring to**
    A. the eternal life of all believers.
    B. the spiritual life of those who were living then.
    C. believers in the tribulation.
    D. believers who are alive when He comes to take them home to heaven.

8. **Jesus' reaction to the sorrow and weeping of His friends was to**
    A. weep as well, as He felt helpless to do anything else.
    B. groan and weep over the effects of sin on humanity.
    C. reprimand them for their lack of trust.
    D. immediately call for Lazarus to come out of the tomb.

9. **The fact that Lazarus had been in the tomb four days is mentioned twice in the narrative. Why is this important?**
    A. It proves that Lazarus really had died.
    B. It establishes the distance that Jesus had to travel to get to Bethany.
    C. It shows how long Mary and Martha had been grieving.
    D. It corroborates the Jewish burial traditions.

10. **Caiaphas prophesied that**
    A. the Romans would be conquered by the Jews.
    B. all the followers of Jesus would desert Him.
    C. Jesus would fall sick and die.
    D. it was expedient that Jesus die for the nation.

What Do You Say?

How would you answer Jesus' question in John 11:26?

_____

_____

_____

_____

LESSON 4

Jesus Enters Jerusalem

John 12

"Let her alone" (12:1-8)

In spite of the many opposed to Christ, there were a few who were true to Him. He enjoyed sweet fellowship with Lazarus, Mary, and Martha at their home in Bethany, but in coming to Bethany at this time He was exposing Himself to danger, because nearby Jerusalem was headquarters for all the forces that were plotting against Him.

Several instances are recorded in the Gospels where Jesus was anointed by a woman. No two incidents are exactly alike, and it is not necessary to conclude that this anointing by Mary is recorded anywhere else. Mary's devotion to Christ caused her to take this pound of very costly ointment and anoint His feet (12:3). She was conveying that nothing was too valuable to give to Him. He is worthy of everything that we have and are.

> **Nothing is too valuable to give to Christ. He is worthy of everything that we have and are.**

Each time we meet Mary she is at the feet of Jesus. Here she is wiping His feet with her hair. A woman's hair is her glory, so she was, as it were, laying her glory at His feet. Needless to say, Mary would have carried the fragrance of the ointment for some time after this. Thus when Christ is worshiped, the worshipers themselves carry away something of the fragrance of that moment. No house is so filled with pleasant odor as the house where Jesus is given His rightful place.

In verse 4, the flesh is seen intruding into this most sacred of occasions. Judas could not stand to see precious ointment used in this way. He did not consider Jesus to be worth three hundred pence. In his opinion, the ointment should have been sold and given to the poor. This was sheer hypocrisy, as he cared no more for the poor than he did for Jesus. He was about to betray the Lord, not for three hundred pence, but for a tenth of that amount. Someone has summarized it in this way: "That anyone could follow Christ as a disciple for three years, see all His miracles, hear all His teaching, receive at His hand repeated kindnesses, be counted an apostle, and yet prove rotten at heart in the end, all this at first sight appears incredible and impossible! Yet the case of Judas shows plainly that the thing can be. Few things, perhaps, are so little realized as the extent of the fall of man." John is quick to add that Judas did not protest this "waste" because he loved the poor, but because he was a thief. He carried the bag for the disciples as their treasurer and took care of their finances, such as they were.

> **Spiritual opportunities are passing. We should never delay doing what we can for the Savior.**

The Lord answered in verse 7, "Do not prevent her from doing this. She has kept this ointment for the day of My burial. Now she wants to lavish it on Me in an act of affection and worship. She should be permitted to do so." There would never be a time when there would not be poor people on whom others might lavish their kindness. But Christ's ministry on earth was swiftly drawing to a close. Mary would not always have the opportunity to minister to Him. Surely this should remind us that spiritual opportunities are passing. We should never delay doing what we can for the Savior.

"On account of [Lazarus] ... many ... believed in Jesus" (12:9-11)

The word quickly spread that Jesus was near Jerusalem. It was no longer possible to keep His presence secret. Many Jews came to Bethany to see Him, and others came to see Lazarus, whom He had raised from the dead.

So insane is the hatred of the human heart, the chief priests were plotting the death of Lazarus. It was as if he had committed high treason by being raised from the dead! They considered him worthy of death because through him many people believed in Jesus. Lazarus was therefore an enemy to the Jewish cause, and he must be put out of the way. Those who bring others to Christ are often made the target for persecution and even martyrdom. (There is no biblical record of the plot against Lazarus actually being carried out.)

"Hosanna!" (12:12-19)

We now come to the triumphal entry of Jesus into Jerusalem. It took place on the Sunday before His crucifixion. It is difficult to know exactly what the crowds thought about Jesus. Did they really understand He was the Son of God and the Messiah of Israel? Or did they merely look upon Him as a king who would deliver them from Roman oppression? Were they carried away with the emotion of the hour? No doubt some in the group were true believers, but the general impression is that most of the people had no real heart interest in Jesus. The palm branches they waved are a token of rest and peace after sorrow (cf. Rev. 7:9). The word *hosanna* means "Save now, we pray You." Thus we can infer that the people were acknowledging Jesus to be the One sent from God to save them from Roman cruelty and to give them rest and peace after the sorrow of their long years of Gentile oppression.

Jesus entered the city riding on a young donkey (12:14). In doing so He was fulfilling prophecy. John quoted from Zechariah 9:9 to prove this—"Fear not, daughter of Zion: behold, your King comes, sitting on a donkey's colt." "The daughter of Zion" is a figurative reference to the Jewish people, Zion being a hill in the city of Jerusalem. The disciples did not realize that what was happening was an exact fulfillment of Zechariah's prophecy—that Jesus was actually entering Jerusalem as the rightful King of Israel. But after Jesus had gone back to heaven to be glorified at the right hand of the Father, it dawned on them that these events were a fulfillment of the Scriptures.

Verses 17 and 18 tell us more about the crowd: that some who watched Jesus enter Jerusalem had witnessed Him raising Lazarus from the dead. These told the others about that amazing miracle. As the report spread, a great throng of people came forth to meet Jesus. Unfortunately, their motive stemmed from curiosity rather than true faith. The Pharisees expressed their frustrations among themselves (12:19); it seemed that nothing they could say or do was having the slightest effect. With a sweeping gesture they cried out that the whole world had gone after Him. They did not realize that the interest of the crowd was just a passing thing, and that those who truly worshiped Jesus as the Son of God were very few in number.

"Sir, we wish to see Jesus" (12:20-26)

Charles Erdmann makes this insightful comment about these next verses: "From among all the memorable incidents of the Passion Week, only one is selected by John; it is recorded by no other writer, but it is distinctly in accordance with the purpose of this Gospel." And Leon Morris further notes:

> In this Gospel we see Jesus as the world's Savior, and evidently John means us to understand that this contact with the Greeks ushered in the climax. The fact that the Greeks had reached the point of wanting to meet Jesus showed that the time had come for him to die for the world. He no longer belongs to Judaism, which in any case has rejected him. But the world, whose Savior he is, awaits him and seeks for him.

The Greeks who came to Jesus at this time were Gentiles who were probably in Jerusalem for Passover because they had become converts to Judaism. No reason is given why they approached Philip in particular. Maybe his Greek name and the fact that he was from Bethsaida of Galilee made him more approachable to these Gentile proselytes. Their request in verse 21 was noble indeed: "Sir," they said, "we wish to see Jesus." One simple principle from this verse is that no one with this desire is ever turned away; one lesson is that Philip's action exemplifies what Christ's disciples should be doing even today—bringing people to Jesus.

The Lord's answer in verse 23 at first seems irrelevant to the Greeks' request. Some have suggested that since the Greeks as a nation were interested in self-culture, self-advancement, and self-enjoyment, Christ was intimating that their philosophy was directly opposed to the law of harvest. Some say that in responding to their desire for Him to come and teach *them* (in the face of the Jews' hostility to Him, cf. 7:35), Christ was conveying here that the blessings they sought could only be acquired by His going to the cross and dying for them.

Seed never produces grain until it has fallen into the ground and died. The Lord here referred to Himself in verse 24 as a grain (corn, or kernel) of wheat. If He did not die, He would abide alone—that is, He would enjoy the glories of heaven by Himself; there would be no saved sinners there to share His glory. But if He died, He would provide a way by which many (including Gentiles) might be delivered into His glory.

The same principle applies to us, as T. G. Ragland says:

> If we refuse to be corns of wheat—falling into the ground, and dying; if we will neither sacrifice prospects, nor risk character, and property, and health; nor, when we are called, relinquish home, and break family ties, for Christ's sake; *then we shall abide alone.* But if we wish to be fruitful, we must follow our Blessed Lord Himself, by becoming a corn of wheat, and dying, *then we shall bring forth much fruit.*

The Lord continues in verse 25: many people think that what's important in life are material and temporal things. They live for these things and fail to realize the soul is more important than the body. By neglecting their soul's welfare, they "lose" their lives. On the other hand, there are those who count all things loss for Christ. They forego things highly prized among men in order to serve Him. These are the people who keep their lives unto life eternal. To hate one's life means to love Christ more than one loves his own interests. To serve Christ, one must follow Him. His servants must obey His teachings and resemble Him morally (12:26). They must apply the example of His death to themselves. He promises throughout His constant presence and protection, not only in the present life but throughout eternity as well. The service we give now will receive God's approval in a coming day. Whatever one suffers of shame or reproach here will seem small indeed when compared with the glory of being publicly commended by God the Father in heaven.

> **To hate one's life means to love Christ more than one loves his own interests. To serve Christ, one must follow Him.**

"For this purpose I came to this hour" (12:27-36)

Increasingly now the Lord's thoughts were on soon-coming events. He was thinking of the cross and contemplating the time when He would become the Sin Bearer. Thinking of the hour of His crucifixion, His soul was troubled. How should He pray in such a moment? Should He ask His Father to save Him from the hour? No! He had come into the world for this very purpose. He had been born to die. So He prayed that the name of His Father might be glorified. He was more interested that honor should come to God than in His own comfort or safety. God now spoke from heaven, proclaiming that He *had* glorified His Name and would glorify it again. The name of God had been glorified by the earthly ministry of Jesus. The thirty silent years in Nazareth, the three years of public ministry, the wonderful words and works of Christ Jesus—all of these glorified the name of the Father. But still greater glory would be brought to God through His death, burial, resurrection, and ascension.

We read in verse 29 that some of those standing by mistook the voice of God for thunder. Some people are always trying to put a natural explanation on spiritual things. Those who are unwilling to accept the fact of miracles try to explain them away by some natural law. Others knew it was not thunder, yet they did not recognize it as the voice of God. Realizing it must have been super-human, they could only conclude it was the voice of an angel. God's voice can only be heard and understood by those who are helped by the Holy Spirit. People can listen to the gospel over and over and never grasp its message unless the Holy Spirit speaks to them through it. Jesus explained to the listeners that the voice did not need to be audible in order for *Him* to hear it; it was made audible for the sake of those who were standing by.

Jesus Speaks of His Crucifixion

"Now is the judgment of this world," He said in verse 31. The world was about to crucify the Lord of life and glory. In doing so, it would condemn itself. Sentence would be passed upon it for its awful rejection of the Christ, God's Anointed One. Condemnation was about to be passed on guilty mankind. The prince of this world is Satan. He thought he had succeeded in doing away with the Lord Jesus. Instead, Jesus provided a way of salvation for all people, and at the same time He defeated Satan and all his hosts. The sentence of doom has not been carried out on the devil as yet, but his doom has been sealed, and it is just a matter of time before he will be cast into the lake of fire.

The first part of verse 32 refers to Christ's death on the cross. He was nailed to a cross of wood and lifted up from the earth. If He were thus crucified, He said, He would "draw all peoples" to Him. The crucifixion of Jesus Christ has resulted in people from all over the world being drawn to Him from every nation, tribe, and language.

In verse 33 Jesus spoke of being "lifted up"; this signified the kind of death He would die, namely, death by crucifixion. John is once again drawing the reader's attention to the omniscience of the Lord. Jesus knew in advance He would be crucified. The people were puzzled by this statement, however. They knew He claimed to be the Messiah, and the Old Testament taught that the Messiah would live forever (see Isa. 9:7; Ps. 110:4; Dan. 7:14; Mic. 4:7). Notice the people quoted Jesus as saying, "The *Son of Man* must be lifted up." Actually, He had said, "*I*, if *I* am lifted up from the earth." All four gospels record the Lord often referring to Himself as the Son of Man (cf. 8:28), so it was not difficult for the people to put the two thoughts together.

> **The crucifixion of Jesus Christ has resulted in people from all over the world being drawn to Him.**

Jesus reminded these people that "the light" would be with them only for a short while. They should come to the Light and walk in it; otherwise darkness would come upon them and they would stumble about in ignorance. Jesus was apparently likening Himself to the sun and the daylight it offers. The sun rises in the morning, reaches its peak at noon, and descends over the horizon in the evening. It is only with us for a limited number of hours. We should avail ourselves of it while it is here because when the night comes, we do not have the benefit of it. The one who believes in Christ is the one who walks in the light. The one who rejects Him walks in darkness and does not know where he is going. He therefore stumbles through life. Again Jesus warned His listeners to put their faith in Him while there was still opportunity (12:36). They would then become children of the light and be assured of direction through life and into eternity. After speaking these words, Jesus departed from the people and remained in obscurity for a while.

"But ... they did not believe in Him" (12:37-43)

John now comments that although Jesus had performed so many mighty works, the people did not believe in Him. Their unbelief was not due to lack of evidence. Jesus had given the most convincing proofs of His deity, but the people did not want to believe. They wanted a king to rule over them, but they did not want to repent (cf. Matt. 4:17). This unbelief was a fulfillment of Isaiah 53:1. The question, "Lord, who has believed our report?" calls for the answer, "Not many." The "arm of the Lord" speaks of the mighty power of God revealed only to those who believe the report concerning the Christ. Because not many accepted the announcement concerning the Messiah, the power of God was not revealed to many.

The Lord Jesus presented Himself to Israel over and over again, yet the nation rejected Him. This illustrates the principle that the more people reject the gospel, the harder it becomes for them to receive it. God causes them to be smitten with "judicial blindness," that is, a blindness which is God's judgment upon them for refusing His Son. In verse 40 John quoted from Isaiah 6:9 and 10. God blinded the eyes of the people of Israel and hardened their hearts—not at first, but only after they had closed their own eyes and hardened their own hearts. As a result, they cut themselves off from sight, understanding, conversion, and healing. The quotation is from the memorable chapter in which Isaiah saw the glory of God. John explains that it was Christ's glory Isaiah saw, and it was of Christ that he spoke. Thus, verse 41 is another link in the chain of evidence that proclaims Jesus to be God.

It might seem strange to us, but we read in verse 42 that many of the chief rulers of the Jews became intellectually convinced that Jesus was the Messiah, but they did not dare to share their conviction with the others in case they were excommunicated. Perhaps these men were genuine believers in the Lord Jesus, but it is extremely doubtful. Where there is true faith, there will be confession of Christ sooner or later. When a person really receives Christ as Lord, he or she makes it known, regardless of the consequences. These men were more interested in the approval of their peers than in the approval of God. They thought more of man's praise than of God's. Can a person like this really be a genuine believer in Christ? See chapter 5, verse 44 for the answer.

"He who believes in Me ..." (12:44-50)

Let us paraphrase verse 44—"The one who believes in Me actually believes not only in Me but also in My Father who sent Me." Here again the Lord taught His absolute union with the Father. It was impossible to believe in one without believing in the other. In one sense, no man can see God the Father; He is spirit, and therefore invisible. But Jesus came to reveal what God is like—not physically, of course, but morally. He has revealed to us the character of God. Therefore, whoever has seen Christ has seen God the Father.

The illustration of light was apparently one of Christ's favorites. Here in verse 46, He again referred to Himself as a light coming into the world so that anyone who believes in Him should not remain in darkness. Apart from Christ, we are in deepest darkness. We do not have a right understanding of life, death, or eternity. But those who come to Christ in faith no longer grope about for the truth because they have found the truth in Him. The purpose of Christ's coming was not to condemn, but to save. He did not sit in judgment on those who refused to hear His words or to believe on Him. This does not mean that He will not judge these unbelievers in a coming day, but that judgment was not the object of His first advent (coming). So far as the coming judgment day is concerned, those who refuse His words will stand before God, and Christ's words—His teaching—will be enough to condemn them.

"I have not spoken on My own authority," He said in verse 49. The things He taught were not things He had made up Himself or learned in a school. He had spoken those things that the Father commissioned Him to speak. This is what will condemn human beings at the last day. The word Jesus spoke comprised God's message, and people refused to hear it. The Father had told Him not only what to say but what He should speak. There is a difference. The expression "what I should say" refers to the substance of the message. The words "what I should speak" refer to the very words that Jesus used in teaching the truth of God. Jesus knew the Father had commissioned Him to give everlasting life to those who would believe on Him. Therefore, He delivered the message as it was given Him by the Father.

> **The purpose of Christ's coming was not to condemn, but to save.**

LESSON 4 EXAM

Use the answer sheet that has been provided to complete your exam.

1. **Judas objected to Mary's use of the precious ointment on Jesus because**
   A. he was a thief and wanted to sell it and keep the profits for himself.
   B. he wanted to sell it and give the money to the poor.
   C. he knew Jesus was going to die soon and wouldn't care about being anointed.
   D. he assumed the others felt the same way and was speaking for them all.

2. **How did Jesus justify Mary's action?**
   A. "She has kept this ointment for the day of My burial."
   B. "The poor are not as important as I am."
   C. "I'm sure we are all enjoying this wonderful fragrance."
   D. "This is part in the hospitality that Mary and Martha are offering."

3. **The chief priests plotted the death of Lazarus because**
   A. he was instigating an uprising.
   B. he told everyone what death was like.
   C. he was talking against the Jewish religion.
   D. on account of him, many believed in Jesus.

4. **The word "Hosanna" means**
   A. "Hail to the King."   C. "Save now."
   B. "Praise the Lord."   D. "Hallelujah."

5. **Jesus was fulfilling a prophecy in the book of _____ when He entered Jerusalem riding on a young donkey.**
   A. Isaiah   C. Zechariah
   B. Micah   D. Malachi

6. **In response to the Greeks' desire to see Him, Jesus spoke of the necessity of His death. How did He illustrate this?**
   A. Time moves along hour by hour, and now was the hour for Him to die.
   B. A grain of wheat must fall into the ground and die in order to produce fruit.
   C. He was the main branch on the vine of Israel and He must be cut off for the nation to survive.
   D. The soil of those who heard His words needed to be tilled and turned in order to be fruitful.

7. **What was Jesus' prayer as He contemplated His soon-coming crucifixion?**
   A. "Father, save me from this hour."
   B. "Father, make My disciples understand."
   C. "Father, glorify Your name."
   D. "Father, change the attitude of the Jews."

8. **The ruler of this world that Jesus speaks of in verse 31 is**
   A. Jesus Himself.   C. Pilate.
   B. Caesar.   D. Satan.

9. **"Judicial blindness" is that blindness which**
   A. causes some men to be born blind.
   B. God imposes as an act of judgment on the hearts of those who refuse to believe in Christ.
   C. causes some people to lose their sight as a result of disease or old age.
   D. afflicts all people who are born in the world as sinners.

10. **The purpose of Christ's first coming was to**
    A. condemn people.   C. save people.
    B. teach people.   D. argue with people.

EXAM 4

What Do You Say?

Draw one lesson from this passage and the course material that you think is especially relevant to young people.

_____

_____

_____

_____

Jesus Sets an Example of Humble Servanthood

John 13

W e now come to a distinct break in the narrative. Up to this point, the Lord has presented Himself to Israel. John has recorded seven distinct signs, or miracles. It is instructive to note how each one illustrates an experience that will result when a sinner puts his faith in Christ. The signs are:

1. *The changing of water into wine* (2:1-12). This pictures the sinner as a stranger to divine joy being transformed by the power of Christ.
2. *The healing of the nobleman's son* (4:46-54). This pictures the sinner as sick and in need of spiritual health.
3. *The healing of the cripple at the pool of Bethesda* (chapter 5). The sinner is without strength, helpless, and unable to do anything to remedy his condition. The Lord Jesus cures him of his infirmity.
4. *The feeding of the five thousand* (chapter 6). The sinner is without food, hungry, and in need of that which not only imparts strength but satisfies. The Lord Jesus provides food for his soul that fully satisfies.
5. *The calming of the Sea of Galilee* (6:16-21). The sinner is in a place of danger—eternal damnation. Christ Jesus rescues him from the storm.

6. *The healing of a man blind from birth* (chapter 9). This pictures man's spiritual blindness until touched by the power of Christ. Man cannot see his own sinfulness, or the beauties of the Savior, until he is enlightened by the Holy Spirit.
7. *The raising of Lazarus from the dead* (chapter 11). The sinner is dead in trespasses and sins and needs life from above.

In chapter 13, Jesus begins to give what is commonly termed "the Upper Room Discourse." Jesus is now no longer walking among the hostile Jews. He has retired with His disciples to an upper room in Jerusalem for a final time of fellowship with them before going forth to His trial and crucifixion. The portion from chapter 13 through chapter 17 is one of the best loved sections in the entire New Testament.

"Jesus ... laid aside His garments" (13:1-11)

It was the day before His crucifixion. Jesus knew the time had come for Him to die, to rise again, and to go back to heaven. He had loved His own—that is, those who had truly believed in Him. He loved them to the end of His earthly ministry, and He will continue to love them throughout eternity. He also loved them to an infinite degree, as He was about to demonstrate.

The expression "supper being ended" (NKJV, 13:2) is not accurate. It should be "during supper" or "while the supper was taking place." Although the text does not specify which supper is referred to here, it is commonly assumed that it is the Passover meal. During the supper, Satan sowed the thought in Judas's mind that the time was ripe to betray Jesus. Judas had plotted against Him long before this, but now he began to put his evil plans into action.

Inspired by the divine Author of Scripture, John records that Jesus was very conscious of the work that had been committed to Him by God, that He had come from God the Father, and that He was returning to Him (13:4). Being conscious of these things, He stooped down and washed the disciples' feet. Rising from supper, He laid aside the long outer garment He was wearing and put a towel around His body as an apron, assuming the role of a slave. This symbolic act reminds us of how the Lord laid aside His heavenly glory, came down into the world as a Servant, and humbly served those He had created. When He completed His task, He took His garments and sat down again in His rightful place (cf. 13:12; compare with Philippians 2:1-11).

The open sandals, so common in eastern lands, made it necessary to wash one's feet frequently. It was common courtesy for a host to provide a slave to wash the feet of his guests. Here, the divine Host became the slave and performed this lowly service. Peter was shocked. He expressed disapproval that One as great as the Lord should condescend to one as unworthy as he.

Jesus used Peter's interruption to reveal that there was a spiritual meaning to what He was doing: foot-washing was a picture of spiritual washing. Peter knew the Lord was performing the physical act, but he did not realize the spiritual significance. He would know it soon, however, for the Lord explained it. And he would know it by experience when later he was restored to the Lord after having denied Him.

Peter illustrates the extremes of human nature. In verse 8 he vowed that the Lord would never wash his feet—and "never" means "not for eternity." The Lord answered Peter that apart from His washing his feet, there could be no fellowship with Him. Bible scholars offer a variety of interpretations as to the meaning of foot washing, one being that it pictured "family forgiveness" for sins that "hinder the believer's fellowship with God" (Constable), and another that it symbolizes "the daily consecration of the disciple's life to a service of love, following Christ's example" (Edersheim).

This author's view is that this spiritual cleansing takes place through the "water," as it were, of the Word. As Christians walk through this world, they become defiled by sin. We need to be constantly cleansed. We read and study the Bible, we hear it preached, we discuss it one with another—and it cleanses us. If we neglect the Bible, sinful influences remain in our minds and lives defiling us and rendering us insensitive to sin. Jesus said to Peter, "You have no part with Me," that is, fellowship with the Lord can remain unhindered only by the continual cleansing action of the Scriptures.

> **The Lord came as a Servant to humbly serve those whom He had created.**

Verse 9 records Peter shifting to the other extreme. A minute earlier he said, "Never." Now he says, "Wash me all over." In His reply, Jesus used two different words for "wash," so what He really said was this: "He who is bathed needs only to wash his feet, but is completely clean." There is a difference between the bath and the basin. The *bath* speaks of the cleansing we receive at the time of salvation. Cleansing from the *penalty* of sin through the blood of Christ takes place only once. The *basin* speaks of cleansing from the *pollution* of sin and must take place continually through the Word of God. We need one bath but many foot cleansings. "You are clean, but not all of you," added Christ. The disciples had received the bath of regeneration—that is, all but Judas. Knowing all things, the Lord knew Judas would betray Him, so He singled out one as never having had the bath of redemption.

"Do as I have done to you" (13:12-20)

It seems that Christ graciously washed the feet of *all* the disciples. Then He put on His outer garments and sat down to explain the spiritual meaning of what He had done. He opened the conversation by asking a question. (Christ's questions make an interesting study; they form one of His most common methods of teaching.) The disciples had acknowledged Jesus to be their Teacher and Lord, and they were right in doing so. If the Teacher and Lord had washed the disciples' feet, what excuse could they have for not washing one another's feet? The basic lesson is, they were to humbly serve one another.

But did the Lord mean they should literally wash each other's feet with water? Was He instituting an ordinance for the church here? No, the meaning here was spiritual. In line with the previous interpretation, they were to keep each other clean by having constant fellowship over the Word. If one sees his brother growing cold or worldly, he should lovingly exhort him from the Holy Scriptures.

Verse 15 tells us that the Lord had given them an object lesson, an example of what they should do to one another in the spiritual realm. If pride or personal animosities prevent us from humbly stooping to serve our brethren, we should remember that we are not greater than Christ. He humbled Himself to wash those who were unworthy and unthankful, and He knew that one of them would betray Him. Would you minister in a lowly way to a man you knew was about to betray you for money? Those who were sent (the disciples) should not consider themselves too lofty to do anything that the One who sent them (the Lord Jesus) had done. To know these truths concerning humility, unselfishness, and loving, gracious service is one thing. The real value and blessedness is in doing them.

What Jesus had just been teaching about service did not apply to Judas (13:18). He was not one of those whom Jesus would send throughout the world with the gospel. Jesus knew the Scriptures concerning His betrayal must be fulfilled—such Scriptures as Psalm 41:9. Judas was one who had eaten his meals with the Lord for three years, and yet he "lifted up his heel" against Him—an expression indicating that he betrayed the Lord. In Psalm 41, the betrayer is described by the Lord as "my own familiar friend." Jesus revealed His betrayal to the disciples in advance so that when it came to pass, they would add this fulfilled prediction to the weight of evidence to Christ's deity. The word "he" should be omitted from verse 19. "You may believe that I AM"—one of the many times Christ used the name of Jehovah of the Old Testament.

Thus, fulfilled prophecy is one of the great proofs of the deity of Christ and also, we might add, of the inspiration of the Scriptures.

> **To know these truths concerning humility, unselfishness, and loving, gracious service is one thing. The real value and blessedness is in doing them.**

In verse 20, because the Lord knew His betrayal might cause the disciples to stumble or doubt, He added a word of encouragement: they should remember they were being sent on a divine mission. They were to be so closely identified with Him that to receive *them* was the same as receiving *Him*. Also, those who received Christ received God the Father.

"One of you will betray Me" (13:21-30)

The knowledge that one of His disciples would betray Him caused Jesus to be deeply stirred. It seems that He was here giving Judas a final opportunity to abandon his plan. Without exposing him directly, Jesus revealed that He knew one of the Twelve would betray Him. But even this did not change the betrayer's mind. The disciples did not suspect Judas. They were surprised that one of their number would do such a thing and puzzled as to who he could be. The words "perplexed about whom He spoke" mean "uncertain of whom He spoke."

In those days, people did not sit up at a table for a meal—they reclined on low couches. The "disciple whom Jesus loved" was John, the writer of this gospel (13:23). He does not mention his name, but does mention the special affection Jesus had for him. Jesus loved all the disciples, but John enjoyed a special sense of closeness to Him. Peter probably used some kind of sign rather than speaking audibly. Perhaps by nodding with his head he asked John to find out the name of the betrayer. In verse 25 we see John leaning back on Christ's breast and asking the fateful question. Probably he spoke in a whisper and was answered in a low tone as well.

Jesus said He would give a piece of bread dipped in wine or meat juice to the traitor (13:26). Some say that an Eastern host gave this piece of bread to the honored guest at a meal. By making Judas the honored guest, Jesus thus tried to win him to repentance. Others suggest that the bread was commonly passed in this way in connection with the Passover supper. If so, then evidently Judas left during the Passover supper and before the Lord's Supper (Matt. 26:26-28) was instituted.

The devil had already put it into Judas's heart to betray the Lord. Now we read in verse 27 that Satan entered into him. At first it was a suggestion, but Judas entertained it, liked it, and agreed to it. Now the devil took control of him. Knowing the betrayer was now fully determined, the Lord told him to do it quickly. Obviously He was not encouraging him to do evil but expressing sorrowful resignation.

Verse 28 confirms the fact that the conversation between Jesus and John was not heard by the other men. They still did not know that Judas was about to betray their Lord. Some of them thought Jesus was telling Judas to go quickly and buy something for the feast. Others thought that, because Judas was the treasurer, Jesus had instructed him to make a donation to the poor. When Judas left, John remarks that "it was night." As well as being night literally, it was night spiritually for Judas—a night of gloom and remorse that would never end. It is always night when men and women turn their backs on the Savior.

"A new commandment I give to you" (13:31-35)

As soon as Judas left, the Lord began to speak with the disciples more freely and intimately. The tension was gone. "Now the Son of Man is glorified," He said. Jesus was anticipating the work of redemption He was about to accomplish. His death might have seemed like defeat, yet it was the means whereby lost sinners might be saved. It was followed by His resurrection and ascension, and He was greatly honored in it all. "And God is glorified in Him."

The work of the Savior brought great glory to God. It proclaimed Him to be a holy God who could not pass over sin, yet also be a loving God who took no pleasure in the death of the sinner; it proclaimed how He could be a just God yet able to justify sinners. Every attribute of deity was magnified at Calvary. Verse 32 starts, "If God is glorified in Him." The "if" here does not express any doubt; it means "since": "Since God is glorified in Him." "God will also glorify Him in Himself," that is, God will ensure that appropriate honor is given to His beloved Son. "And glorify

Him immediately." He will do it without delay. The Father fulfilled this prediction by raising the Lord Jesus from the dead and seating Him at His own right hand in heaven. He would not wait until the kingdom was ushered in; He would glorify His Son immediately.

At this point, Jesus addressed His disciples as little children—a term of endearment (13:33). Notice He used it only after Judas had departed. He was only to be with them for a little while. Then He would die on the cross. They would seek Him then, but would not be able to follow Him, for He would return to heaven. Jesus had told the same thing to the Jews, but He meant it in a different sense. For the disciples, His departure would only be temporary. He would come again for them. But for the Jews, His leaving would be final. He was returning to heaven, and they could not follow Him because of their unbelief.

> **His death might have seemed like defeat, yet it was the means whereby lost sinners might be saved.**

During His absence, the disciples were to be governed by the commandment of love (13:34). This commandment was not new inasmuch as the Ten Commandments taught love for God and for one's neighbor, but it was new in other ways: Jesus had given a living demonstration of it, and the Holy Spirit would empower believers to obey it. It was also new in its superiority to the old; the old said, "Love your neighbor," but the new said, "Love your enemies." It was new in that it called for a higher degree of love: "As I have loved you, that you also love one another."

Verse 35 summarizes a true characteristic of Christian discipleship as love for fellow Christians. This requires divine power, and this power is given only to those indwelt by the Spirit.

"I will lay down My life for Your sake" (13:36-38)

From verse 36 it is clear that Peter did not understand that Jesus had spoken of His death. He thought Jesus was going on some earthly journey, and he did not understand why he could not go along. The Lord told Peter he would follow later (that is, when he died), but could not do so now. With typical devotion and enthusiasm, Peter expressed in verse 37 his willingness to die for his Lord. Jesus checked Peter's "zeal without knowledge" by telling him that before the night was ended, he would deny Him three times. Thus Peter was reminded of his weakness and cowardice, and his inability to follow Christ for even a few hours by his own power.

LESSON 5 EXAM

Use the answer sheet that has been provided to complete your exam.

1. **Chapter 13 begins a section in John's gospel where Jesus**
   A. preaches for the last time to the crowds.
   B. spends time with only His disciples.
   C. prepares His defense for His trial before Pilate.
   D. goes alone to the desert for a time of prayer.

2. **The incident of Jesus washing the feet of His disciples demonstrated**
   A. His humble service in coming to earth to serve mankind.
   B. His wanting to humiliate the disciples for not doing this task themselves.
   C. His desire to institute this practice for the coming church age.
   D. His way of getting the disciples' attention.

3. **The two kinds of washings symbolized**
   A. adult baptism (immersion) and infant baptism (sprinkling).
   B. cleansing of the body and cleansing of the soul.
   C. initial cleansing from sin's penalty and ongoing cleansing from sin's pollution.
   D. cleansing by blood and cleansing by the Spirit.

4. **How can Christians be cleansed from the sinful defilement of the world?**
   A. By staying away from things of the world.
   B. By singing hymns to keep our focus on God.
   C. By going to church as often as we can.
   D. By submitting to the cleansing action of the Word of God.

5. **"If pride or personal animosities prevent us from humbly stooping to serve our brethren, we should remember that**
   A. pride was the chief sin of Satan, and repent of it."
   B. we are not greater than Christ."

C. Christ taught we should do to others what we want them to do for us."

D. pride comes before a fall."

6. **Psalm 41:9 was fulfilled when**
   A. Judas betrayed the Lord Jesus.
   B. the Romans crucified Jesus.
   C. Caiaphas prophesied Jesus' death.
   D. Peter denied knowing Jesus.

7. **The Lord indicated the identity of His betrayer by**
   A. naming him openly before all the disciples.
   B. giving him a piece of bread dipped in sauce.
   C. whispering his name to John.
   D. nodding in his direction.

8. **Both Jesus and God the Father would be glorified by His death in that**
   A. it showed the reliability of the Roman justice system.
   B. it showed God's control over the actions of men.
   C. it was the means by which lost sinners might be saved.
   D. nature would react to the traumatic event.

9. **The new commandment Jesus gave to the disciples was**
   A. to abolish the Sabbath and keep Sunday as sacred.
   B. to live in poverty the rest of their lives.
   C. to continue to obey the Law with greater motivation.
   D. to love one another as He had loved them.

10. **When Peter expressed his willingness to die for Jesus if necessary, Jesus told him,**
    A. "I appreciate your willingness, but it won't be necessary."
    B. "You don't know what you are talking about."
    C. "The rooster will not crow till you have denied Me three times."
    D. "I was born to die, and now is the time."

EXAM 5

What Do You Say?

Share about a time when you served others and experienced the "blessing" (John 13:17) of doing so.

_____

_____

_____

_____

Jesus Is the Way, the Truth, and the Life

John 14

"I am the way, the truth, and the life" (14:1-14)

Although some think that Jesus spoke the opening verse of chapter 14 as a continuation of the last verse of the previous chapter (remember, chapter breaks were created centuries after the Scriptures were penned), He was undoubtedly addressing all the disciples, as the pronouns "your" and "you" are plural. The thought seems to be this: "I am going away, and you will not be able to see Me. But do not let your heart be troubled. You believe in God in spite of the fact that you do not see Him; now believe in Me in the same way." Once again, John draws the reader's attention to another of Christ's claims to equality with God.

> It was to Calvary that the Lord Jesus went to prepare a place for His own people.

In verse 2 the Father's house refers to heaven, where there are many dwelling places—in other words, there is room there for all the redeemed. If it were not so, Jesus would have said so; He would not have them build on false hopes. "I go to prepare a place for you," He said. It was to Calvary that the Lord Jesus went to prepare a place for His own people. It is through His atoning death that believers are assured of a place with Him in heaven. As someone has wisely commented, "God is not in the construction business in heaven!" It was at Calvary that He made provision in His heavenly home for His people.

Verse 3 refers to the time when Jesus Christ will come in the air, when those who have died in faith will be raised, when the living will be changed, and when all the blood-bought throng will be taken home to heaven (1 Thess. 4:13-18; 1 Cor. 15:51-58). This is a personal, literal coming of Christ. As surely as He went away, He will come again. His desire is to have His own with Him for all eternity (John 17:24).

Jesus Declares He Is the Way to God

A more accurate translation of verse 4 is: "And where I go, you know the way." He was going to heaven, and they knew the way to heaven for He had told them many times. Apparently Thomas did not understand the meaning of the Lord's words. Like Peter, he may have been thinking of a journey to some place on earth. Jesus explained that He Himself is the way to heaven. He does not merely show the way; He *is* the way. Salvation is in a person. Accept that person as your own and you have salvation. Christianity is Christ. The Lord is the truth. He is not just One who

> Jesus explained that He Himself is the way to heaven. He does not merely show the way; He *is* the way.

teaches the truth; He *is* the truth. He is the embodiment of truth. Those who have Christ have the truth. It is not found anywhere else.

Christ Jesus is the life. He is the source of life, both spiritual and eternal. Those who receive Him have eternal life because He is the life. No one comes to the Father except by Him. The way to God is not by keeping the Ten Commandments, the Golden Rule, ordinances, or having church membership—it is by Christ, and Christ alone. Many say that it does not matter what a person believes as long as he is sincere. They say all religions have some good in them and they all lead to heaven at last. But Jesus said, "No one comes to the Father except through Me."

Jesus Reaffirms His Unity with the Father

Once more (14:7), the Lord emphasized the mysterious union that exists between the Father and Himself. If the disciples had recognized who Jesus really was, they would have known the Father also, because Jesus revealed the Father to human beings (1:18). From now on, and especially after Christ's resurrection, the disciples would understand that Jesus was God the Son. Then they would realize that to know Christ was to know the Father, and to see Christ was to see God. This verse does not teach that

God and Jesus Christ are the same person; there are three distinct persons in the Godhead, but there is only one God.

Philip, in verse 8, requested some special revelation of the Father. He did not understand that everything the Lord was, and did, and said was a revelation of the Father.

The Lord patiently corrected him. Philip had been with Him a long time; he was one of the first disciples Jesus had called (1:43). Yet the full truth of Christ's deity and of His unity with the Father had apparently not yet dawned on him. He did not know that when he looked at Jesus, he was looking upon One who perfectly displayed the Father. The Lord's words "I am in the Father, and the Father in Me" describe the closeness of the union between the Father and the Son. They are separate Persons and yet are one as to attributes and will.

We should not be discouraged if we cannot understand this. No mortal mind will ever understand the Godhead. We must give God credit for knowing things we can never know. If we fully understood Him, we would be as great as He! Some words must be supplied in the latter part of this verse to complete the meaning. We might paraphrase it as follows: "The words that I speak to you, I do not speak by My own authority, but the Father who dwells in Me, He speaks the words; and the works that I do, I do not do them on My own initiative, but the Father who dwells in Me is the One who performs these miracles." Jesus had power to speak the words and to do the miracles, but He came into the world as Jehovah's Servant, and He spoke and acted in perfect obedience to the Father. The disciples should have believed that He was one with the Father simply because of His own testimony to that fact. But if that wasn't enough, then the miracles He performed should have prompted them to believe it.

Jesus Explains Future Miracles

Jesus then predicted that they would perform miracles like He did, and even greater miracles (14:12). In the book of Acts we read of the apostles performing miracles of bodily healing similar to those of Christ's. But we also read of greater miracles—such as the conversion of 3000 on the day of Pentecost. It was to the world-wide proclamation of the gospel, the salvation of many souls, and the building of the church that Jesus referred by the expression "greater works." It is greater to save souls than to heal bodies. It was through the power of the Holy Spirit that the apostles performed these greater miracles subsequent to His coming upon them at Pentecost.

What a comfort it must have been to the disciples to know that, even though Christ was leaving them, they could pray to the Father in His name and receive their requests (14:13). We must be careful to interpret this verse in its context—it does not mean that a believer can get anything he wants from God. The key to the promise is in the words "in My name." "Whatever you ask in My name …" To ask in Jesus' name is not simply to insert the phrase "in Jesus' name" at the end of the prayer; it is to ask in accordance with His mind and will. It is to ask for those things that will glorify God, bless mankind, and be for our own spiritual good. In order to ask in Christ's name, we must live in close fellowship with Him—otherwise, we would not know His attitude. The closer we are to Him, the more our desires will be the same as His. The Father is glorified in the Son because the Son only desires those things that please God. As prayers of this nature are presented and granted, God receives great glory. The promise is repeated for emphasis and as a strong encouragement to God's people. Live in the center of God's will, walk in fellowship with Christ, ask for those things that Christ would desire, and your prayers will be answered.

"The Holy Spirit … will teach you all things" (14:15-26)

The Lord Jesus was about to leave His disciples, and they would be filled with sorrow. The way they should express their love for Him was by keeping His commandments. Not by weeping, but by obeying. The commandments of the Lord are the instructions He has given us that we read in the Gospels, as well as all the other writings of the New Testament.

It is interesting to note in verse 16 that when the word "pray" is used of Jesus, it is not the word sometimes used to describe an inferior praying to a superior—it is the word that describes a person making a request of his equal. The Lord would pray the Father to send another Helper. The word "Helper" means one who comes to the side of another to help. It is also translated Advocate and Comforter. The Lord Jesus is our Helper, Advocate, or Comforter, and the Holy Spirit is another Helper—not another of a different kind, but another of similar nature, the same kind. The Holy Spirit would abide with believers forever. In the Old Testament, the Holy Spirit came upon men and women at various times, but often left them. Now it would no longer be so; He would come to remain forever.

The Holy Spirit is called "the Spirit of truth" because His teaching is true and He glorifies Christ who is the truth (14:17). The world cannot receive the Holy Spirit because it cannot see Him. Unbelievers want to see before they will believe. The unsaved do not know or understand the Holy Spirit. He may convict them of sin, and yet they do not know that it is He. The disciples knew the Holy Spirit. They had known His work in their own lives, and had seen Him working through the Lord Jesus. "He dwells with you and will be in you," said Jesus. Since Pentecost, when a person believes on the Lord Jesus, the Holy Spirit takes up His abode in that person's life forever. King David's prayer to God, "Do not take Your Holy Spirit from me" (Ps. 51:11), would not be suitable today. The Holy Spirit is never taken from a believer, although He might be grieved, and quenched, and hindered.

Christ assured His disciples He would not leave them as orphans, or desolate.

Christ assured His disciples He would not leave them as orphans, or desolate (14:18). He would come again to them. He appeared to them, of course, after His resurrection, but it is doubtful if that is what He meant. In another sense, He came to them in the person of the Holy Spirit on the day of Pentecost. In a third sense, He will come to them again in a literal manner at the end of this age, when He will take His chosen ones home to heaven.

No unbeliever saw the Lord Jesus after His burial (14:19). After He was raised, He was seen only by those who loved Him. But even after His ascension, His disciples continued to see Him by faith. This is what is meant by the words "but you will see Me." In the promise "Because I live, you will live also," the Lord was looking forward to His resurrection life that would be the pledge of life for all who would put their trust in Him. Although they would die, they would be raised again to die no more. The expression "at that day" in verse 20 probably refers again to the descent of the Holy Spirit. He instructs us that just as there was a vital link between the Son and the Father, so there would be a marvelous union of life and interests between Christ and His people. It is difficult to explain how Christ is in the believer and the believer in Christ at the same time. A poker can be in the fire and the fire in the poker, but this does not fully illustrate the concept. Christ is in the believer in the sense that His life is communicated to him or her. He actually dwells in the believer through the Holy Spirit. The believer is in Christ in the sense that he stands before God in all the merit of the person and work of Christ.

Jesus Explains the Results of Obedience

In verse 21, we see that the real proof of one's love for the Lord is obedience to His commandments. The Father loves such. In one sense, the Father loves (has demonstrated compassion for) all people, but He has a special love and affection for those who love His Son. Christ loves them too, and He makes Himself known to them in a special way. The more we love the Savior, the better we shall know Him.

It was the misfortune of the Judas mentioned in verse 22 to have the same name as the traitor. But the Spirit of God inspired John to distinguish him from Iscariot. This Judas could not understand how Jesus could appear to the disciples without also being seen by the world. No doubt he was thinking of Christ's coming as a conquering King. He did not understand that the Lord would manifest Himself to His own in a spiritual manner— that is, they would see Him by faith through the written Word of God. By the Spirit of God, we can actually know Christ better today than the disciples knew Him when He was on earth. Those in the front of the crowd were closer to Him than those in the rear. But today, by faith, each of us can enjoy the closest of fellowship with Him.

> **The real proof of one's love for the Lord is obedience to His commandments.**

If a person truly loves the Lord Jesus Christ, he will want to obey all His teachings, not just isolated commandments (14:23). The Father loves those who are willing to obey His Son without questions or reservations. Both Father and Son are especially near to such loving and obedient hearts. On the other hand, those who do not love Him do not keep His sayings. And they are not only refusing the words of Christ, but those of God the Father as well (14:24).

While He was with them, our Lord taught His disciples up to a certain point, but He could not reveal more truth to them because they could not take it in (14:25). The Holy Spirit would, however, reveal more. The Spirit was sent by the Father in the name of Christ on the day of Pentecost. He came to represent Christ's interests on earth. He did not come to glorify Himself, but to draw men and women to the Savior. "He will teach you all things," said Jesus. He did this first of all through the spoken ministry of the apostles, then through the written New Testament. The Holy Spirit would bring to remembrance all that Christ had taught. The Lord presented all the teaching that is developed by the Holy Spirit in the rest of the New Testament.

"Peace I leave with you" (14:27-31)

A person about to die usually writes a last will and testament in which he leaves his possessions to his loved ones. Here the Lord Jesus was doing that very thing. However, He did not bequeath material things, but something that money could not buy—*peace,* inward peace of conscience that arises from a sense of pardoned sin and reconciliation with God. Christ can give it because He purchased it with His own blood at Calvary. He does not give it as the world gives—sparingly, selfishly, and for a short time. His gift of peace is forever. Why then should a Christian be troubled or afraid?

Jesus had already told the disciples He was going to leave them and then return later to take them to heaven. If they loved Him, He said, this would cause them to rejoice (14:28). Of course, in a sense they did love Him. But they did not fully appreciate who He was, and thus their love was not as great as it should have been. "You would rejoice because I said, 'I am going to the Father,' for My Father is greater than I." At first it seems as if this verse contradicts all that Jesus had taught concerning His equality with God the Father. But there is no contradiction, and the passage explains the meaning. When Jesus was here on earth, He was hated and hunted, persecuted, and pursued. Men blasphemed Him, reviled Him, and spat on Him. He endured terrible indignities from the hands of His creatures. The Father never suffered such rude treatment from human beings. He dwelt in heaven, far away from the wickedness of sinners.

When Christ returned to heaven, He would be where indignities could never come. Therefore, the disciples should rejoice when He said that He was going to the Father, because in this sense the Father was greater than He. The Father was not greater *as God,* but greater because He never came into the world as a man to be cruelly treated. As far as the attributes of deity are concerned, the Son and the Father are equal. But when we think of the lowly place which the Son took as a human being here on earth, we realize that in that sense,

> Christ's gift of peace is forever. Why then should a Christian be troubled or afraid?

God the Father was greater than He. In unselfish concern for the fearful disciples, Jesus revealed these future events to them so that they would not be offended, disheartened, or afraid, but believe in all He had told them.

From verse 30, we see that the Lord knew the time for His betrayal was drawing near and that He would not have much more time to talk with His own. Satan was coming, but Jesus knew the enemy could find no taint of sin in Him.

We might paraphrase verse 31 as follows: "The time of My betrayal is very near. I will go voluntarily to the cross. This is the Father's will for Me. It will convey to the world how much I love My Father. That is why I am now going without offering any resistance." With this, the Lord bade the disciples to arise and go with Him. It is not clear whether they moved from the upper room at this point. Perhaps the rest of the discourse took place as they walked along.

LESSON 6 EXAM

Use the answer sheet that has been provided to complete your exam.

1. **In verse 1, Jesus was addressing**
   A. only Peter.
   B. specifically John.
   C. mostly Judas.
   D. all the disciples.

2. **Where was it that Jesus was going to prepare "a place" for His followers?**
   A. To the cross of Calvary.
   B. To Bethlehem.
   C. To the temple.
   D. To a different house in which to eat the Passover.

3. **The only way to have a relationship with God is through**
   A. regular church attendance.
   B. Jesus Christ.
   C. keeping the Ten Commandments.
   D. following the Golden Rule.

4. **Jesus explained His unity with the Father as**
   A. "I am the same as the Father."
   B. "I am in the Father and the Father is in Me."
   C. "I will become the same as the Father when I return to heaven."
   D. "I am the Father."

5. **The "greater works" that Jesus said His disciples would do in the future**
   A. were more spectacular types of healings.
   B. were many more instances of raising the dead.
   C. was the world-wide proclamation of the gospel and the salvation of many souls.
   D. was the conversion of the entire Jewish nation.

6. **When praying, to "ask in Jesus' name" means to**
   A. ask in accordance with His mind and will.
   B. add that phrase to the end of the prayer.
   C. be certain that whatever we pray for will be given to us.
   D. begin our prayer with that phrase to get God's attention.

EXAM 6

7. _____ is the way Jesus said we can express our love for Him.
   A. Praying frequently
   B. Using our time in His service
   C. Keeping His commandments
   D. Mourning over His death

8. Jesus promised that when the Holy Spirit came He would
   A. be beside His disciples to help them.
   B. push His disciples in the right direction.
   C. come and go as needed.
   D. abide in His followers forever.

9. One of the Holy Spirit's specific functions for the remaining 11 disciples was to
   A. reward them for staying by Christ's side throughout His public ministry.
   B. protect them from ever being arrested for following Christ.
   C. bring Christ's teachings to remembrance when they penned the New Testament.
   D. give them special powers to win over the Pharisees to Christ.

10. Jesus told the disciples what was about to happen to Him so that
    A. they would help Him face these things with courage.
    B. when it happened, they would believe.
    C. they would find a way to hide Him.
    D. when it happened, they would know how to escape.

What Do You Say?

Which one of the many promises Christ made in this chapter do you especially take to heart today, and why?

_____

_____

_____

_____

Jesus Is the True Vine

John 15

"I am the true vine" (15:1-11)

In the Old Testament, the nation of Israel was depicted as a vine planted by Jehovah. The nation, however, had proved unfaithful and unfruitful, so God the Son, in the person of the Lord Jesus Christ, now presented Himself as the true—the faithful—Vine. God the Father is the Vinedresser (the Farmer, i.e. the One who cares for the vineyard).

Opinions differ as to what Jesus meant by the fruitless branch in verse 2. Some think it is a person who professes to be a Christian but has never really been united to Christ by faith. Others think it is a true Christian who loses his salvation because of his failure to bear fruit. This is clearly impossible because it contradicts so many other passages which teach that the believer's salvation is eternally secure. Others think that it is a true Christian who becomes a backslider. He gets away from the Lord and becomes interested in the things of this world. He fails to manifest the fruit of the Spirit (Gal. 5:22-23). As a result, the Lord chastens him with sickness, sorrow, or, in extreme cases, He removes him from the world because of his poor testimony. The author favors this latter view.

The branch that bears fruit is the Christian who is growing more like Christ. Even such vines need to be pruned. Just as a real vine must be cleansed from insects, mildew, and fungus, so a Christian must be cleansed from worldly things that cling to him (15:3). The cleansing agent is the word (teachings) of the Lord. The disciples had received His word at the time of their individual conversions, and even as Christ was talking to them, His word was having a purifying effect on their lives. Thus, this verse may refer to both justification and sanctification. By extension to us today, all of God's written Word is for our cleansing.

Fruitful Christians Abide in the Vine

In verse 4, the words "to abide" mean to stay where you are. The Christian has been placed in Christ; that is his position. In his daily walk, he should *stay* in intimate fellowship with Christ. A branch abides in a vine by drawing all its life and nourishment from the vine. We abide in Christ by spending time in prayer, reading God's Word, fellowshiping with His people, and being continually conscious of our union with Him. As we thus maintain constant contact with Him, we are conscious of His abiding in us and supplying us with spiritual strength and resources. The branch can only bear fruit as it abides in the vine. The only way believers can bear the fruit of a Christ-like character is by living in touch with Christ.

Christ Himself is the Vine; believers are the branches (15:5). It is not a question of the branch living its life for the Vine, but simply of letting the life of the Vine flow out through the branches. Sometimes we pray, "Lord, help me to live my life for You." It would be better to pray, "Lord Jesus, live out Your life through me." Without Christ, we can do nothing. A vine's branch has one great purpose—to bear fruit. It is useless for making furniture or for building homes. It does not even make good firewood. But it is good for fruit bearing—as long as it abides in the vine.

> **We abide in Christ by spending time in prayer, reading God's Word, fellowship, and being continually conscious of Him.**

Verse 6 is another verse in this passage that has caused much difference of opinion. Many believe that the person described is a believer who falls into sin and is subsequently lost. Such an interpretation directly contradicts many Scriptures which teach that no true child of God will ever perish. Others believe that this person is a professing Christian but was never truly born again. We would like to suggest that this man is a true believer, for it is with true Christians that this section is concerned. The subject of this section is not salvation, but abiding and fruit bearing. This person, through carelessness and prayerlessness, gets out of touch with the Lord. As a result, he commits some sin, and his testimony is ruined. Through failure to abide in Christ, he is cast forth as a branch—not by Christ, but by men. *Men* gather the branches and cast them into the fire, and they are burned. It is not God who does it, or angels, but people. What does this mean? It means that unbelievers scoff and judge this backslidden Christian. They drag his name in the mud. They throw his testimony as a Christian in the fire. This is illustrated in the life of David. He was a true believer, but he became cold in heart toward the Lord and committed the sins of adultery and murder (2 Samuel 11). He caused the enemies of the Lord to blaspheme. They cast him, as it were, into the fire.

Prayerful Christians Abide in the Vine

Verse 7 tells us that the abiding life is the secret of a vibrant prayer life. The closer we get to the Lord, the more we will learn to think His thoughts after Him. The more we get to know Him through His Word, the more we will understand His will. The more our will agrees with His, the more we can be sure of having our prayers answered. Children of God exhibit the likeness of Christ to the world, and the Father is honored (15:8). People are forced to confess He must be a great God when He can transform such wicked sinners into such godly saints. Notice the progression in this chapter: fruit (15:2), more fruit (15:2), much fruit (15:8). "So you will be My disciples." This can hardly mean that we become disciples by abiding in Christ; the way to become a disciple is to believe in the Lord Jesus. It means we are *manifest* as His disciples when we abide in Him. Others can then see that we are true disciples, that we resemble our Lord.

The love which Christ has for us is the same love the Father has for the Son (15:9). How marvelous! Our hearts bow in worship when we read such words. This love is the same in quality and in degree. It is vast, wide, deep, and immeasurable, and it can never be fully comprehended by man. "Abide in My love," said Jesus in verse 9. We should continue to realize His love and to enjoy it. The first part of verse 10 tells how we can continue (or abide) in His love: it is by keeping His commandments. The second half of the verse sets before us the Lord Jesus as our perfect example. He kept His Father's commandments. Everything He did was in obedience to God's will. He remained in the constant enjoyment of the Father's love. Nothing came in to spoil that sweet sense of loving fellowship.

Jesus found His own deep joy in communion with God His Father (15:11). He wanted His disciples to have that joy which comes from dependence upon Him. He wanted His joy to be theirs. Man's idea of joy is to be as happy as he can, leaving God out of his life. Jesus taught that real joy comes by taking God into one's life as much as possible. "That your joy may be full," or better, "fulfilled." Their joy would be fulfilled in abiding in Christ and in keeping His commandments.

"Love one another" (15:12-17)

The Lord was soon to leave His disciples. They would be left in a hostile world. As tensions increased, danger of the disciples contending with one another would be a real possibility. So, in verse 12 Jesus leaves this standing order: "Love one another as I have loved you." They should even be willing to die for one another (15:13). People who are willing to do this do not fight with one another. The greatest example of human self-sacrifice is for a man to die for his friends. Believers are called to this type of devotion. Some lay down their lives in a literal sense; others spend their whole lives in untiring service for the people of God. The Lord Jesus is our ultimate example: He laid down His life for His friends. Of course, we are enemies by natural birth, but when we are saved we become His friends. So it is correct to say He died for His friends as well as for His enemies. We show we are His friends by keeping His commandments (15:14). This is not the way we become His friends, but the way we exhibit this to the world.

In verse 15, Jesus emphasized the difference between a servant and a friend. A servant is simply expected to do work marked out for him, but a friend is taken into one's confidence. To a friend we reveal our plans for the future. Confidential information is shared. In one sense the disciples would always continue to be the Lord's servants, but now they would be more than this—they would be His friends. The Lord was even now revealing to them the things He had heard from His Father. He was telling them of His

> As branches, we receive; as disciples, we follow; and as friends, we commune.

own departure, the coming of the Holy Spirit, His own coming again, and their responsibility to Him in the meantime. Someone has pointed out that as branches, we receive (15:5); as disciples, we follow (15:8); and as friends, we commune (15:15).

In case there should be any tendency for the disciples to become discouraged and give up, Jesus reminded them in verse 16 that He had chosen them with a purpose in mind. He chose them to eternal salvation, to discipleship, and to fruitfulness. Fruit may mean the graces of the Christian life, such as love, joy, and peace. Or it may mean souls won for the Lord

Jesus Christ. There is a close link between the two, for it is only as we are manifesting the first kind of fruit that we will ever be able to bring forth the second. The expression "that your fruit should remain" implies that fruit here means the salvation of souls. The Lord had chosen the disciples to go and bring forth lasting fruit. He was not interested in mere professions of faith in Himself, but in genuine cases of salvation. L. S. Chafer notes that in this chapter we have prayer effectual (15:7); joy celestial (15:11); and fruit perpetual (15:16). "That whatever you ask …" The secret of effective service is prayer. "Asking the Father in prayer—in Jesus' name—was necessary for fruit-bearing to happen. Jesus linked prayer and fruit-bearing in a cause and effect relationship" (Thomas Constable).

The Lord was about to warn the disciples about the enmity of the world. He began as we have seen by telling them in verse 17 to love one another, to stick together, and to stand unitedly against the foe.

"The servant is not greater than his master" (15:18-27)

The disciples were not to be surprised or disheartened if the world hated them (15:18). The word "if" does not express any doubt that this would happen; it may be translated "since," for the hatred of the world for them could be counted on. The world hated the Lord Jesus, and it will hate all who resemble Him. Men and women of the world love those who live as they do, indulging the flesh. A Christian condemns them by his holy life, and so they hate him. The disciple should not expect any better treatment from the world than his Lord received. He will be persecuted just as Christ was. His word will be refused just as Christ's was.

This hatred and persecution is for His name's sake (15:21). It is because the believer is linked to Christ; because he has been separated from the world by Christ; and because he bears Christ's name and likeness. The world is ignorant of God. They do not know that the Father sent Jesus Christ into the world to be the Savior. But ignorance is no excuse.

The Lord was not teaching in verse 22 that if He had not come, there would be no sinners; from the time of Adam, all human beings have been sinners. But their sin would not have been nearly so great as it now was. These men had seen the Son of God and heard His wonderful words. They could find no fault in Him whatever. Yet they rejected Him. It was this that made their sin so great. Thus it was a matter of comparison. Compared with their terrible sin of rejecting the Lord of glory, their other sins were as nothing. Now they had no excuse for their sin. And what's more, in hating

Christ, they also hated the Father (15:23), for the Father and the Son are one. They could not say that they loved God, for if they had, they would have loved Him whom God had sent.

They had not only heard His words, they had seen His works—miracles that no other person had ever performed. And in the face of such evidence to His deity, they still rejected Him. Again, all their other sins were minor compared to this, and they stood condemned (15:24). But notice how the Lord drew the disciples' attention to the fact that man's attitude to Christ had been predicted. The Lord applied Psalm 69:4 to Himself—that He would be hated without any reason. The Lord commented that the very Old Testament Scriptures which these men prized had predicted their hatred of Him. The fact that it was prophesied did not mean that these men *had* to hate Christ; they hated Him by their own deliberate choice, but God foresaw that it would happen, and He caused David to write it in advance.

In spite of man's rejection, there would be a continued testimony to Christ. It would be carried on by the "Helper"—the Holy Spirit. Here the Lord said He would send the Spirit from the Father (15:26). In John 14:16, the Father was the One who sent the Spirit. This is another proof of the equality of the Son and the Father. The Spirit of truth proceeded from the Father. This meant that He was constantly being sent forth by God, and His coming at the day of Pentecost was a special instance of this. The Spirit testifies concerning Christ. This is His great mission. He directs the attention of both sinner and saint to the Lord of glory. The Spirit would witness directly through the disciples. They had been with Jesus from the beginning of His public ministry and were especially qualified to tell of His person and work. If anyone could have found any imperfection in the Lord, it would be those who had been with Him. But they never knew Him to commit a sin of any kind. They could testify to the fact that He was the sinless Son of God and the Savior of the world.

LESSON 7 EXAM

Use the answer sheet that has been provided to complete your exam.

1. **The Lord Jesus presented Himself as the true Vine because**
   A. God had rejected the nation of Israel.
   B. His followers would replace Israel in God's plan.
   C. the nation of Israel, also called a vine, had proved itself to be unfruitful.
   D. His disciples needed a visual image.

2. **The Father uses _____ to prune and cleanse fruit-bearing branches.**
   A. the Scriptures   C. temporary separation
   B. punishment   D. removal of the Holy Spirit

3. **The only way to be a fruitful branch is to**
   A. remove yourself from the world.
   B. overcome evil temptations.
   C. ignore unsaved friends.
   D. abide in Christ.

4. **Being "cast into the fire" is interpreted in the course as**
   A. being cast into the lake of fire.
   B. being "burned" as a result of unrighteous contact with the world.
   C. being judged and denounced by unbelievers.
   D. being disciplined by church elders.

5. **Jesus is our example of how to abide in His love. He abode in His Father's love by**
   A. traveling around teaching people.
   B. keeping His commandments.
   C. performing many miracles.
   D. spending hours in prayer.

6. **As well as being Christ's servants, in this chapter He also calls His disciples**
   A. His apostles.   C. His companions.
   B. His brothers.   D. His friends.

EXAM 7

7. **Jesus reminded His disciples that He had chosen them for a purpose, which was**
   A. to listen to His teaching so they could teach others.
   B. to protect and comfort Him in His coming ordeal.
   C. to go and bear lasting fruit.
   D. to provide the means for His work on earth.

8. **Jesus told His disciples that they would be _____ because that was how the world treated Him.**
   A. respected and honored
   B. hated and persecuted
   C. listened to and followed
   D. loved and sought out

9. **When, speaking of His enemies, the Lord said, "If I had not come and spoken to them, they would have no sin," He meant that**
   A. compared to their sin of rejecting Him, their other sins were insignificant.
   B. they had been born into the world without sin.
   C. if they now accepted who He was, they would no longer be sinners.
   D. if they loved the Father but hated Him, they would have no sin.

10. **The great mission of the Holy Spirit is to**
   A. enable men to speak in tongues.
   B. testify concerning Jesus Christ.
   C. regenerate all mankind.
   D. add new revelations to the Bible from time to time.

What Do You Say?

Comment on the observation in the course about the two prayers, "Lord, help me to live my life for You" and "Lord, live out Your life through me."

Jesus Prepares His Disciples for the Future

John 16

"The time is coming" (16:1-4)

The disciples cherished the current general hope of the Jewish people that the Messiah would set up His kingdom and the power of Rome over them would be broken. Instead of that, the Lord told them He was going to die, rise again, and go back to heaven. The Holy Spirit would come, and the disciples would go out as witnesses for Christ. They would be hated and persecuted. We find in verse 1 that the Lord told them all this in advance so they would not be disillusioned, offended, or shocked.

In verse 2 Jesus continues to tell the disciples what is ahead for them. Excommunication from the synagogue was considered by most Jews to be one of the worst things that could happen. Yet this would happen to these Jews who were disciples of Jesus. The Christian faith would be so hated that those who sought to stamp it out would think they were pleasing God by doing so. This shows how a person may be very sincere and very zealous, and yet be very wrong. Failure to recognize the deity of Christ would be at the root of the matter. The Jews would not receive Him, and in so doing refused to receive the Father. Again the Lord warned the disciples in advance so they would not be moved by these afflictions when they happened. They would remember that He had predicted persecution; they would know that it was all a part of His plan for their lives. He had not told them much about this earlier because He was with them. There was no need to trouble them or to cause their minds to wander from the other things He had to teach them. But now that He was leaving them, He must tell them of the path that lay ahead for them.

"The Spirit of truth … will guide you into all truth" (16:5-15)

In verse 5, Jesus seems to express disappointment that the disciples were not more interested in what was ahead for *Him*. Although they had asked in a general way where He was going, they were more concerned with their own future than with His. Before Him lay the cross and the grave; before them lay persecution in their service for Christ. They were filled with sorrow over their own troubles rather than over His. However, they would not be left without help and comfort. Verse 7 contains the promise of the Holy Spirit. Christ would send the Holy Spirit to be their Helper. It was expedient for the disciples that the Helper should come. He would empower them, give them courage, teach them, and make Christ more real to them than He had ever been before. The Helper would not come until the Lord Jesus went back to heaven and was glorified. Of course, the Holy Spirit had been active in the world before this, but He was coming in a new way—to convict the world and to minister to the redeemed.

The Holy Spirit would convict the world of sin, of righteousness, and of judgment (16:8). This is generally taken to mean that He creates an inward awareness of these things in the life of the individual sinner. While this is true, it is not exactly the teaching in this portion. *The Holy Spirit condemns the world by the very fact of His presence here.* He should not be here; the Lord Jesus should be here, reigning over the world. But the world rejected Him, and He went back to heaven. The Holy Spirit is here in place of a rejected Christ, and thus the world's guilt is demonstrated. The Spirit convicts the world of the sin of failing to believe on Christ, because He was worthy of belief. There was nothing about Him that made it impossible for people to believe in Him. But they refused. And the Holy Spirit's presence in the world is witness to their crime. Christ claimed to be righteous, but men said He had a demon. God spoke the final word. He said, in effect, "My Son is righteous, and I will prove it by raising Him from the dead and taking Him back to heaven." The Holy Spirit witnesses to the fact that Christ was right and the world was wrong. The presence of the Holy Spirit also convicts the world of coming judgment. The fact that He is here means that the devil has already been condemned at the cross and that all who reject Christ will share his awful judgment in a day yet future.

In verse 12 Jesus says there were other things He had to tell the disciples, but they could not take them in. This is an important principle of teaching; there must be progress in learning before advanced truths can be received. The Lord never overwhelmed His disciples with teaching; He gave it to them in doses that they could handle.

In verses 13 to 15 the Lord unveils more of the work of the Holy Spirit. The work which the Lord began was to be continued by the Holy Spirit. He would guide them into "all truth." There is a sense in which "all truth" was committed to the apostles in their lifetime. They, in turn, committed it to the written page, and we have it today in our New Testament. This, added to the Old Testament, completed God's written revelation to man. But it is, of course, true in all ages that the Spirit guides God's people into all the truth. He does it through the Scriptures. "He will not speak on His own authority," said Jesus. This does not mean that He would not speak *about* Himself, but that He would not speak *from* Himself. He would only speak the things given to Him to say by the Father and the Son. "He will tell you things to come." This, of course, is done in the New Testament,

> The Spirit unveils to the believer's heart the glorious perfections, ministries, offices, graces, and fullness of the Lord Jesus Christ.

and particularly in the book of Revelation, where the future is unveiled.

The Holy Spirit's principle work is to glorify Christ. By this we can test all teaching and preaching. If its effect is to magnify Christ, then it is of the Holy Spirit. "He will take of what is Mine" means "He will receive of the great truths that concern Me." These are the things He reveals to believers. The subject can never be exhausted. All the attributes of the Father belong to the Son as well. It is these perfections that Jesus was speaking of in verse 14. The Spirit unveils to the believer's heart the glorious perfections, ministries, offices, graces, and fullness of the Lord Jesus Christ.

"Your sorrow will be turned to joy" (16:16-22)

The meaning of verse 16 is not at all clear. It may mean that the Lord would be away from them for three days, and then He would reappear to them after His resurrection. It may mean He was going back to His Father in heaven, and then after "a little while" (the present age) come back to them (His second coming). Or it may mean that for a little while they would not see Him with their physical eyes, but after the Holy Spirit was given on the day of Pentecost, they would perceive Him by faith in a way they had never seen Him before. (The words "because I go to the Father" should not be included in this verse because they are not found in the best manuscripts.)

The disciples were confused. They could not reconcile these statements, "I go to My Father, and you see Me no more" (16:10) with "A little while, and you will not see Me; and again, a little while, and you will see Me" (16:16). In verse 18 they asked each other the meaning of the words "a little while." We have the same problem. We do not know whether the expression refers to the three days before His resurrection, the forty days before Pentecost, or the almost 2000 years prior to His coming again!

The Lord Jesus, being God, was able to read their thoughts. By His questions, He revealed His full knowledge of their perplexity (16:19). He did not answer their problem directly but gave further information concerning the "little while." For the world, it would be a time of great rejoicing because they would have succeeded in crucifying the Lord Jesus. For the disciples, it would mean weeping and lamentation. But it would only be for a short while. Their sorrow would be turned into joy, and it was—first by the resurrection, and then by the coming of the Spirit. Then, for all disciples of all eras, sorrow will be turned to rejoicing when Christ comes back again. Nothing is more remarkable than the speed with which a mother forgets the pains of childbirth after her child is born. So it would be with the disciples. The sorrow connected with the absence of their Lord would be quickly forgotten when they saw Him again. Once more, we must express ignorance as to the time indicated by the Lord's words, "I will see you again," in verse 22. Does this refer to His resurrection, His sending of the Spirit at Pentecost, or His second advent? In all three cases, the result is rejoicing and a joy that abides.

"Ask and you will receive" (16:23-28)

Up until now, the disciples had come to the Lord with all their questions and requests. In that day (the age ushered in by the descent of the Spirit at Pentecost) He would no longer be with them physically, so they would no longer be able to ask Him questions. But that did not mean they would have no one to whom to go. It would be their privilege to pray to God the Father. He would grant their requests for Jesus' sake. "Whatever you ask the Father in My name He will give you." Requests will be granted not because *we* are worthy, but because God counts His Son worthy. Prior to this, the disciples had never prayed to God the Father in the Lord's name. Now they were invited to do so. Through answered prayer, their joy would be fulfilled.

In verse 25, we read that the meaning of much of the Lord's teaching was not always apparent on the surface. Even in this chapter we cannot always be sure of the precise meaning. With the coming of the Holy Spirit, the teaching concerning the Father became more plain. In the book of Acts and in the Epistles, truth is revealed through direct statements.

In the age of the Holy Spirit (in which we now live), our privilege is to pray to the Father in the name of the Lord Jesus. "I do not say to you that I shall pray [beseech] the Father for you," said Jesus in verse 26. The Father does not need to be urged to answer our prayers. At the same time, however, the Lord Jesus is the Mediator between God and man, and He intercedes on behalf of His people before the throne of God.

> **Our privilege is to pray to the Father in the name of the Lord Jesus.**

The Father loved the disciples because they had received Christ and loved Him and believed in His deity. This is the reason why Christ did not have to beseech the Father. With the coming of the Holy Spirit, the disciples would enjoy a new sense of intimacy with the Father. They would be able to approach Him with confidence, and all because they had loved His Son.

In verse 28, the Lord repeats His claim to equality with God the Father. He did not say "I came forth from God" as if He were just a prophet sent by God, but, "I came forth from the Father." This means He is the eternal Son of the eternal Father, equal with God the Father. He came into the world as One who had lived elsewhere before His coming. At His ascension, He left the world and returned to His Father. In this one verse we have a concise biographical account of the Lord of glory.

"Be of good cheer, I have overcome the world" (16:29-33)

The disciples thought that they were now able to understand Him for the first time. He was no longer speaking in proverbs, they said. They thought they now entered into the mystery of His person. They believed that He had all knowledge and that He came forth from *God*. But He had said that He came forth from the *Father*. Did they understand the meaning of this? Did they understand that Jesus was one of the persons of the Godhead? In verse 31 Jesus suggested that their belief was still imperfect. He knew they loved Him and trusted Him, but did they really know that He was God manifest in the flesh? In a short while He would be arrested, tried, and crucified. The disciples would all forsake Him and flee. But He would not be deserted, because the Father would be with Him. It was this union with God the Father that they did not understand. This was the thing that would support Him when they had all escaped for their lives.

We read in verse 33 that the purpose of this discourse with the disciples was that they might have peace. When they found themselves hated, pursued, persecuted, falsely condemned, and even tortured, they could have peace *in Him.* He overcame the world at the cross of Calvary. In spite of their tribulations, they could rest assured that they were on the winning side. Also, with the coming of the Holy Spirit, they would have new powers of endurance and new courage to face the foe.

LESSON 8 EXAM

Use the answer sheet that has been provided to complete your exam.

1. **Jesus told His disciples about their future so that**
    A. they could move to another country and avoid it.
    B. they could prepare how to defend themselves.
    C. they would not be shocked or disheartened when it happened.
    D. they had time to reassess whether following Christ was worth it.

2. **The attitude of those who would persecute Christ's followers was**
    A. they really believed they were serving God in doing this.
    B. they knew Jesus' claims were true, but decided to stamp out His influence anyway.
    C. they wanted to take over as leaders in this new religion.
    D. they were afraid of them.

3. **It was to the advantage of the disciples that Jesus would go away because**
    A. then they would be able to travel about more freely.
    B. then He would send the Holy Spirit as their Helper.
    C. then they would be able to spend more time with their families.
    D. they were becoming too dependent on Him.

4. **The role of the Holy Spirit in relation to the world is to**
    A. disdain it and only occupy Himself with the welfare of the disciples.
    B. erode its power till Jesus returns.
    C. force all people to acknowledge that Jesus is God.
    D. convict and condemn it for rejecting Christ.

5. **The Holy Spirit's function with believers is to**
    A. make sure they are obedient to the commandments.
    B. punish them when they disobey.
    C. teach them, especially about the person and work of Christ.
    D. set up local churches all over the world.

6. **The joy of seeing Christ again is compared to**
    A. the joy of a father reconciling with an errant child.
    B. the joy of a new mother after the pain of giving birth.

EXAM 8

C. the joy of reaping bountiful crops despite a year of drought.

D. the joy of completing a difficult job and being rewarded for it.

7. **Now that the Holy Spirit has come, believers are instructed to**
   A. pray to the Father in Jesus' name.
   B. pray to the Father in the Holy Spirit's name.
   C. pray directly to the Holy Spirit.
   D. pray directly to Jesus in heaven.

8. **One of Jesus' own assertions to His deity is seen in**
   A. His reference to His preexistence with God in heaven.
   B. His performance of another sign in their presence.
   C. His reading the thoughts of all the disciples.
   D. His explanation of His virgin birth.

9. **Who did Jesus say was going to be the only one to not desert Him?**
   A. His mother.
   B. John, the beloved disciple.
   C. Mary, sister of Martha and Lazarus.
   D. His Father.

10. **Christ's overall intent in this discourse was that His disciples would have**
    A. love for one another.
    B. peace, assured of His victory over the world.
    C. emotional strength to endure the coming few days.
    D. insight into the plan of God to save sinners.

What Do You Say?

What have you learned about the Holy Spirit's work that encourages your spirit?

_____

_____

_____

_____

Jesus Prays for His Own

John 17

W̲e come now to what is known as the high-priestly prayer of the Lord Jesus. In this prayer, He makes intercession for His own. It is a picture of His present ministry in heaven where He is praying for His people. As Marcus Rainsford put it:

> The whole prayer is a beautiful illustration of our blessed Lord's intercession at the right hand of God. Not a word against His people; no reference to their failings, or their shortcomings; no allusion to what they had done; none to what they were about to do as a body—'They all forsook Him and fled.' No. He speaks of them only as they were in the Father's purpose, as in association with Himself, and as the recipients of the fullness He came down from heaven to bestow upon them.
>
> Observe that all the Lord's particular petitions for His people relate to spiritual things; all have reference to heavenly blessings. The Lord does not ask riches for them, or honours, or worldly influence, or great preferments, but He does most earnestly pray that they may be kept from evil, separated from the world, qualified for duty, and brought home safely to heaven. Soul prosperity is the best prosperity: it is the index of true prosperity.

"O Father, glorify Me together with Yourself" (17:1-5)

The hour had come. Many times His enemies had been unable to take Him because His hour had not come. But now the time had arrived for the Lord Jesus Christ to be put to death. "Glorify Your Son," Jesus prayed. He was looking ahead to His death on the cross. Were He to remain in the grave, the world would know He was just another man. But if God glorified Him by raising Him from the dead, it would be proof He was God's Son and the world's Savior. God answered this request.

The Son Glorified the Father

"That Your Son also may glorify You," the Lord continued. The meaning of this is explained in verses 2 and 3. The Lord Jesus glorifies the Father by giving eternal life to those who believe in Him. It brings great glory to God when ungodly men and women are converted and manifest the life of the Lord Jesus on earth. As a result of His work of redemption, God has given His Son authority over all mankind. This authority entitles Him to give eternal life to those whom the Father has given to Him. Before the foundation of the world, God marked out certain ones as belonging to Christ. Remember, though, that God offers salvation to anyone who will receive Christ. There is no one who cannot be saved by trusting Him. Eternal life is only obtainable by knowing the only true God (in contrast to idols, which are not genuine gods at all) and the Lord Jesus Christ. The name of Jesus Christ is mentioned together with God the Father's as being the joint source of eternal life—yet another testimony in this gospel of their equality in the Godhead. Notice how the Lord spoke of Himself: "Jesus Christ." As you know by now, the word "Christ" is the same as "Messiah." Here John is recording another instance where Jesus asserted His messiahship.

> The Lord Jesus glorifies the Father by giving eternal life to those who believe in Him.

When Jesus uttered the words in verse 4, "I have glorified You on the earth: I have finished the work which You have given Me to do," He was speaking as if He had already died, been buried, and risen again. He had glorified the Father by His sinless life, by His miracles, by His suffering and death, and by His resurrection. He had finished the work of salvation the Father had given Him to do. As someone has said,

The crucifixion brought glory to the Father. It glorified His wisdom, faithfulness, holiness, and love. It showed Him wise, in providing a plan whereby He could be just and yet the justifier of the ungodly. It showed Him faithful in keeping His promise, that the seed of the woman should bruise the serpent's head. It showed Him holy, in requiring His law's demands to be satisfied by our great Substitute. It showed Him loving, in providing such a Mediator, such a Redeemer, and such a Friend for sinful man as His co-eternal Son.

The crucifixion brought glory to the Son. It glorified His compassion, His patience, and His power. It showed Him most compassionate, in dying for us, suffering in our stead, allowing Himself to be counted sin and a curse for us, and buying our redemption with the price of His own blood. It showed Him most patient, in not dying the common death of most men, but in willingly submitting to such pains and unknown agonies as no mind can conceive, when with a word He could have summoned His Father's angels, and been set free. It showed Him most powerful, in bearing the weight of the sin of the world, vanquishing Satan, and despoiling him of his prey.

The Father Glorified the Son

Before Christ came into the world, He dwelt in heaven with the Father (17:5). When the angels looked upon Jesus Christ, they saw all the glory of Deity. To every eye, He was obviously God. But when He came among men, the glory of Deity was veiled. Though He was still God, it was not apparent to most onlookers. They saw Him merely as the carpenter's son. Here the Lord Jesus is praying that the visible manifestation of His glory in heaven might be restored. The words "Glorify Me together with Yourself" mean "Glorify Me with Your presence in heaven. Let the original glory which I shared with You before My incarnation be resumed." This clearly conveys the fact of His pre-existence.

"I pray ... for those whom You have given Me" (17:6-19)

Jesus had manifested the Father's name to the disciples. In Scripture, a person's name reflects his personality, attributes, and character. Christ had fully declared the Father (17:6; cf. 1:18). The disciples had been given to the Son out of the world. They were separated from the unbelieving mass of mankind and set apart to belong to Christ. "They have kept Your word." In spite of all their failures and shortcomings, He credits them with having believed and obeyed His teaching—not a word, as observed above, of their failings. What grace!

Christ had perfectly represented His Father; He had explained to the disciples that He did not speak or act by His own authority, but only as the Father instructed Him. So they knew that the Father had sent the Son. Moreover, Christ did not originate His own mission. He came in obedience to the Father's will; He was the perfect Servant of Jehovah.

As High Priest, He prayed for His followers, not for the world. Here in verse 9 He was praying as the One who represents believers before the throne of God, and His prayer there can only be for His own.

Jesus Is Glorified in the Disciples

The perfect union between the Father and the Son is shown in verse 10. No mere man could truthfully say these words. We might be able to say to God, "All mine are Yours," but we could not say, "All Yours are mine." It is because the Son is equal with the Father that He could make such a statement. In this whole section He presents His poor and backward flock and, as if He was displaying them in a robe of many colors, declares, "I am glorified in them."

In verse 11, again the Lord Jesus anticipates His return to heaven. He prays as if He is already there. His request for His people was that they might be kept by the Father as a united people. He knew they would be subjected to terrible temptations and persecutions. There would be the danger of their being divided and driven apart. So Jesus prayed that "they may be one, as We are." He wanted them to enjoy the same unity in fellowship that exists between the Father and Himself. Notice the title "Holy Father": "Holy" conveys He is *infinitely high*; "Father," that He is *intimately nigh* (near).

While He was with the disciples, Christ kept them in the Father's name (that is, by His power and authority) and true to Him. "None of them is lost," said Jesus, "except the son of perdition," referring to Judas. Judas was not one of those given to the Son by the Father. The term "the son of perdition" means Judas was destined to eternal damnation. Judas was not compelled to betray Christ in order to fulfill prophecy, but he chose to betray Christ, and in so doing he fulfilled Scripture.

The Lord now explained (17:13) why He was praying in the presence of His disciples. It was as if He said to them: "These are intercessions which I shall never cease to make in heaven before God; but I make them now in the world, in your hearing, that you may more distinctly understand how I am to be employed there in promoting your welfare, so that you may be made in large measure partakers of My joy." The Lord had given God's "word"—message—to the disciples, and they had embraced it. As a result, the world turned on them and hated them. They had the characteristics of the Lord Jesus, and so the world hated them. They did not fit in with the world's scheme of things. The Lord does not want the Father to take believers home to heaven immediately; they must be left here to grow in grace and to witness for Christ. His prayer is that they might be kept from the evil one. Not escape, but preservation. The Christian is not "of the world," even as Christ was not of the world, and he should remember this when tempted to engage in some worldly pastime or enter into worldly associations where the name of Jesus is unwelcome.

> **Believers are to represent God to the world. It is for this reason that Jesus sent them into the world.**

To "sanctify" in verse 17 means to set apart. The message Christ communicated from His Father has a sanctifying effect on believers. As they read it and obey it, they are set apart as vessels that are fit for the Master's use. That is exactly what the Lord Jesus was praying for here. He wanted a people who were set apart to God from the world and usable by God. "Your word is truth," Jesus said—not "Your word *contains* truth," but "Your word *is* truth."

The Father sent the Son into the world to reveal the character of God to humankind (17:18). But the Son would soon be going back to heaven. Future generations would still need some witnesses concerning God. This work must be done by believers, through the power of the Holy Spirit. Christians can never represent God as perfectly as the Lord Jesus did because they can never be equal with God. But just the same, believers are here to represent God to the world. It is for this reason that Jesus sent them into the world.

To sanctify does not necessarily mean to make holy. Jesus Christ *is* holy as to His personal character, yet here in verse 19 He says, "I sanctify Myself." The thought is that He *set Himself apart* for the work His Father sent Him to do. The thought may also be that He set Himself apart by taking His place outside the world and entering into the glory. "His sanctification is the pattern of, and the power for, ours," says Vine. We should be set apart from the world and find our portion with Him.

"I do not pray for these alone" (17:20-26)

From verse 20 onwards, the High Priest now extended His prayer beyond the disciples. He prayed for generations yet unborn. In fact, everyone who is a believer can say as he reads this verse, "Jesus prayed for me." The prayer was for unity among believers, but this time it was with the salvation of sinners in view (17:21). Between the Father and the Son there is unity of life and purpose. Believers have the life of Christ and should thus act in harmony with the Lord and with one another. This verse does not teach that the entire world will believe—but Christians, by a united testimony, should present a strong inducement for belief. When Christ comes back with His saints, and this unity is visibly displayed, the world will then know that the Father sent Him. But in the meantime, we should be seeking to demonstrate this truth.

In verse 11, the Lord prayed for unity in fellowship. In verse 21, He prayed for unity in witness-bearing. Now, in verse 22, He prays for unity in glory. This looks forward to the time when saints will receive their glorified bodies. "The glory which You gave Me" is the glory of resurrection and ascension.

We do not have this glory yet. It has been given to us as far as the purposes of God are concerned, but we will not receive it until the Lord takes us to heaven. It will be manifested to the world when Christ returns to set up His kingdom on earth. At that time, the world will realize the vital unity between the Father and the Son, and the Son and His people, and will realize (too late) that Jesus was the Sent One from God. The world will not only realize that Jesus was God the Son but will also know that believers were loved by God just as Christ was loved by God. That we should be so loved seems almost incredible, but it's true!

What a great promise we see in verse 24: the Son desires to have His people with Him in glory. Every time a believer dies, this prayer is answered.

If we realize this, it will comfort us in our sorrow. To die is to go to be with Christ and to behold His glory. This glory is not only the glory of Deity which He had with God before the world began, it is also the glory He acquired as Savior and Redeemer. The glory is a proof that God loved Christ before the foundation of the world.

The world failed to see God as revealed in Jesus Christ (17:25). But a few disciples did, and they believed that God had sent Him. On the eve of His crucifixion, there were only a few of all mankind who really knew Him—and even those were about to forsake Him.

The Lord Jesus had declared the Father's name to His disciples when He was with them. In other words, He had revealed the Father to them. His words and works were the words and works of the Father. They saw in Christ a perfect expression of the Father. The Lord Jesus has continued to declare the Father's name through the ministry of the Holy Spirit. Ever since Pentecost, the Spirit has been teaching believers

That we should be so loved seems almost incredible, but it's true!

about God the Father (especially through the written Word, the Bible). When men and women accept the Father as He is revealed by the Lord Jesus, they become special objects of the Father's love. Since the Lord Jesus indwells all believers, the Father can look upon them and treat them as He does His only Son. Reuss remarks, "The love of God which, before the creation of the physical world, had its adequate object in the person of the Son, finds it, since the creation of the new spiritual world, in all those who are united with the Son." And Godet adds, "What God desired in sending His Son here on earth was precisely that He might form for Himself in the midst of humanity a family of children like Him."

It is because the Lord Jesus is in the believer that God can love him as He loves His Son.

LESSON 9 EXAM

Use the answer sheet that has been provided to complete your exam.

1. **This prayer of the Lord Jesus in John 17 is often called His**
   A. prayer of agony.
   C. Magnificat.
   B. high priestly prayer.
   D. last will and testament.

2. **This prayer**
   A. focused on spiritual blessings for His people, not material ones.
   B. shows His disciples up for the unspiritual men they were.
   C. rehearses the many good works Jesus had done.
   D. reveals God's plan for Christ's second coming.

3. **How would God the Father glorify His Son in His death?**
   A. By giving Him a world-wide following.
   B. By honoring His disciples with the Jewish leaders.
   C. By setting up His earthly kingdom within five years.
   D. By raising Him from the dead.

4. **How would God the Son glorify His Father?**
   A. By giving eternal life to those who believe on Him.
   B. By proclaiming from the cross who God really is.
   C. By not complaining about the treatment He was given.
   D. By appearing to the Pharisees after He rose from the dead.

5. **In His prayer, Jesus described His disciples to God this way:**
   A. "They kept Me company."
   B. "They tried hard, but often failed to do what I told them."
   C. "They have kept Your word."
   D. "They are My friends."

6. **Jesus described His followers as**
   A. being too good for the world.
   B. just as bad as everyone in the world.
   C. belonging to the world.
   D. not being of the world.

7. **Jesus said in His prayer that the means of sanctification from the world and for service is**
   A. fasting.
   B. God's word.
   C. fellowship with other Christians.
   D. a devoted prayer life.

8. **In addition to praying for the Eleven, Jesus also prayed specifically for**
   A. the men who would put Him to death.
   B. all who would ever believe through the testimony of these men.
   C. the Jewish nation as a whole.
   D. His unbelieving family.

9. **The unity of believers is intended to promote _____ in unbelievers.**
   A. fear
   B. belief in Christ
   C. hostility
   D. tolerance

10. **Which specific prayer of the Lord Jesus is answered every time a believer in Him dies?**
    A. Their sins are forgiven.
    B. They are given rewards for their service for Christ.
    C. They are reunited with their deceased believing loved ones.
    D. They go to be with Christ where He is.

EXAM 9

What Do You Say?

How has Christ's prayer that His followers be sanctified by God's word been answered in your life?

Jesus Is Arrested and Tried

John 18

"Shall I not drink the cup which My Father has given Me?" (18:1-11)

Jesus spoke the words of chapters 13–17 in Jerusalem. Now He and the Eleven left the city and walked eastward toward the Mount of Olives. He crossed the brook Kidron and came to the Garden of Gethsemane, which was on the western slope of the Mount of Olives. Judas knew that Jesus spent a great deal of time in this place with His disciples (18:2). With a band of soldiers and officers from the chief priests and Pharisees, Judas came to Gethsemane. The band of men was probably a group of Roman soldiers; the officers were Jewish officials, representing the chief priests and Pharisees. They came with lanterns and torches and weapons. As someone has observed, "They came to seek the Light of the world with lanterns."

In verse 4 we read that Jesus took the initiative and went forth to meet them, without waiting for them to find Him. This demonstrated both His willingness to go to the cross and the fact that He was in complete control of the situation—a further mark of His deity. The soldiers could have left their weapons at home; the Lord would not resist. "Whom are you seeking?" He asked. The question was to draw from their own lips the nature of their mission. They sought Jesus of Nazareth, and He responded "I am." (The "He" is not found in the original.) He was Jesus of Nazareth; He was Jehovah as well. For a brief moment, Jesus revealed Himself to them as the I AM, the Almighty God. It appears that the revelation was so overpowering that they were driven back and fell to the ground. Again Jesus asked them whom they sought. And the answer was the same, despite the effect which two words of Christ had just had upon them. Once more, Jesus told them that He was the One they sought and that He was Jehovah. "I have told you that I am," He said. Since they were only seeking Him, they should let the disciples go. It is wonderful to see His unselfish interest in others at a time when His own life was in peril. Thus, too, the words of John 17:12 were fulfilled.

Peter thought the time had come to save his Master from the crowd by violence (18:10)—he drew his sword and struck the servant of the high priest. Undoubtedly he intended to kill him, but the sword was deflected, so it only cut off the servant's right ear. Jesus rebuked Peter's ill-advised zeal. The cup of suffering and death had been given to Him by His Father, and He intended to drink it. Luke tells us how the Lord touched and healed the ear of Malchus at this point, performing His final public miracle (Luke 22:51).

"They led Him away" (18:12-14)

Now, for the first time, wicked men are able to lay hold of the Lord Jesus and bind Him. He was taken away to Annas, the previous high priest. (This incident was not recorded in the other gospels.) It is not clear why Jesus should have been brought to him first rather than to Caiaphas, his son-in-law, who was now high priest. What is important is that Jesus was first put on trial before the Jews in an attempt to prove Him guilty of blasphemy and heresy. That was what we might call a *religious* trial. Later He was taken to be tried before the Roman authorities in an attempt to prove He was an enemy of Caesar. That was the *civil* trial. Since the Jews were under Roman rule, they had to work through the Roman courts— they could not carry out the death penalty themselves. That had to be done by Pilate.

John notes that the high priest was the same Caiaphas who had prophesied that one man should die for the nation (11:50). He was now about to have part in the fulfillment of the prophecy.

> This was the man who was the accredited guardian of the nation's soul. He had been set apart to be the supreme interpreter and representative of the Most High. To him was committed the glorious privilege of entering once every year into the holy of holies. Yet this was the man

who condemned the Son of God. History provides no more startling illustration of the truth that the best religious opportunities in the world and the most promising environment will not guarantee a man's salvation or of themselves ennoble his soul. "Then I saw," says John Bunyan, closing his book, "that there was a way to hell, even from the gates of heaven."

–James Stewart

"And Peter stood with them and warmed himself" (18:15-18)

Most Bible scholars believe that "the other disciple" mentioned here in verse 15 was John, but that humility prevented him from mentioning his own name, especially in view of Peter's shameful failure. We are not told how John knew the high priest—he may have been related to him—but it was his connection with the high priest that gained him admittance to the palace, or court. Peter was not allowed entry until John went out and spoke to the woman who was the doorkeeper. Looking back, we wonder if it was a kindness for John to use his influence in this way.

Peter's first denial of Christ was not before a soldier, but a simple servant girl. When asked, he denied that he was a disciple of Jesus. Peter now mingled with the enemies of his Lord and tried to conceal his identity. Like many other unwise disciples, he warmed himself at this world's fire and would eventually get "burned."

"I spoke openly to the world" (18:19-24)

Annas questioned Jesus concerning His disciples and His teachings. They had no real case against Him and were trying to make one up. The Lord answered in verse 20 that His ministry had been public; He had nothing to hide. He had taught in the presence of the Jews in synagogues and in the temple. There was no secrecy. He challenged His judges to bring forward Jews who had listened to Him. Let them bring charges against Him. If He had done or said something wrong, let the witness be brought. The reply irritated His hostile audience. It left them without a case, so they resorted to abuse. One of the officers slapped Jesus for speaking to the high priest in such a manner. With perfect poise and logic, Christ showed the injustice of their position. They could not accuse Him of speaking evil, yet they struck Him for telling the truth.

Annas now sent Jesus the prisoner to Caiaphas. The trial before Caiaphas is not described in John's gospel; it took place between verses 24 and 28 of this chapter.

"... and immediately a rooster crowed" (18:25-27)

The narrative now turns back to Peter. In the cold of the early morning hours, he warmed himself by the fire. No doubt his clothing and his accent indicated that he was a Galilean fisherman. The man standing with him asked if he was a disciple of this Jesus. He denied the Lord again. Then a relative of Malchus spoke to Peter. He had seen him cut off his relative's ear. "Didn't I see you in the garden with this Jesus?" he said. For the third time, Peter denied knowing the Lord. Immediately, he heard the crowing of a rooster and was reminded of Christ's words, "The rooster shall not crow till you have denied Me three times." We know from the other gospel accounts that Peter went out at this point and wept bitterly.

"I find no fault in Him at all" (18:28-40)

The religious trial was ended, and the civil trial was now about to begin. The scene is the hall of judgment in the governor's palace. The Jewish leaders did not want to go into the palace of a Gentile—to do so would be to defile themselves, preventing them from eating the Passover. It did not bother them that they were plotting the death of the Son of God! Augustine remarks,

> O impious blindness! They would be defiled, forsooth, by a dwelling which was another's, and not be defiled by a crime which was their own. They feared to be defiled by the praetorium of an alien judge, and feared not to be defiled by the blood of an innocent brother.

Poole comments, "Nothing is more common than for persons overzealous about rituals to be remiss about morals." (The expression "But that they might eat the Passover" probably means the feast which followed the Passover, as the Passover itself had been held the previous night.)

Jesus Is Tried Publicly by Pilate

We see in verse 29 that Pilate, the Roman governor, yielded to the religious scruples of the Jews by going out to where they were. He began the trial by asking them to state the charge against the prisoner. Their answer was bold and rude. They said in effect that they had already tried the case and found Him guilty; all they wanted Pilate to do was to pronounce the sentence. We see in verse 31 Pilate trying to evade responsibility and throw it back on the Jews. If they had already tried Jesus and found Him guilty, why did they not sentence Him according to their law? The Jews said, in reply, "We are not an independent nation. We have been taken over by the Roman power. Civil government has been taken from our hands, and we no longer have the authority to put a person to death." They thus confessed their bondage and subjection to a Gentile power. Moreover, they wanted to shift the infamy of Christ's death to Pilate.

Verse 32 may have two different meanings. (1) In Matthew 20:19, Jesus had predicted that He would be delivered up to the Gentiles to be killed. The Jews were fulfilling His word. (2) On several occasions, Jesus had said He would be "lifted up" (3:14; 8:28; 12:32, 34). This referred to death by crucifixion. The Jews used stoning in cases of capital punishment, whereas the Roman method was crucifixion. By refusing to carry out the death penalty, the Jews unknowingly fulfilled these two prophecies concerning Christ. (See also Psalm 22:16.)

Jesus Is Tried Privately by Pilate

Pilate now took Jesus into the palace for a private interview and asked Him point blank—"Are you the King of the Jews?" Jesus answered in verse 34 in effect, "As governor, have you ever heard that I tried to overthrow Roman rule? Has it ever been reported to you that I proclaimed myself a king who would undermine Caesar's empire? Is this charge something you know by personal experience, or is it what you have just heard these Jews saying?" Pilate's reply in verse 35 was contemptuous, "Am I a Jew?" he said, implying he was too important to be troubled with such a local Jewish problem. But his answer was also an admission that he knew of no real charge against Jesus; he only knew what the rulers of the Jews had said. Jesus then confessed He *was* a king—but not the kind of king the Jews accused Him of being, and not the kind that would threaten Rome.

Christ's kingdom is not advanced by human weapons—otherwise His disciples would have fought to prevent His capture by the Jews. Christ's kingdom is "not from here." It is not of this world; it does not receive its power or authority from the world; its aims and objectives are not related to this world.

In verse 37 Pilate next asked Him if He was indeed a king. Jesus answered, "You say rightly that I am a king." This was simply a form of saying, "Yes, what you say about Me is true." But His kingdom is concerned with truth, not with swords and shields. It was to bear witness to the truth that He came into the world. The truth here means the truth about God, about Christ Himself, the Holy Spirit, man, sin, salvation, and all the other great doctrines of Christianity. Those who loved the truth heard His voice, and that is how His "empire" grew. Pilate asked, "What is truth?" It is difficult to discern what he meant here. Was he puzzled, or sarcastic, or interested? All we know is that Truth Incarnate stood before him, and he did not recognize Him as such. Pilate hurried to the Jews with the admission that he could find no fault in Jesus (18:38).

> **Christ's kingdom is not of this world; it does not receive its power or authority from the world.**

From verse 39 we learn that it was the custom at Passover time for the Jews to request the release of some notorious Jewish prisoner from the Romans. Pilate seized upon this custom in an effort to please the Jews and at the same time set Jesus free. The plan failed. The Jews chose a notorious rebel, murderer, and robber named Barabbas to be released over the holy and harmless Messiah.

LESSON 10 EXAM

Use the answer sheet that has been provided to complete your exam.

1. **Jesus and His disciples left Jerusalem and walked to**
    A. Bethany.
    C. Galilee.
    B. Gethsemane.
    D. Bethlehem.

2. **Judas came to find Jesus**
    A. with a group of soldiers.
    B. by himself.
    C. with a group of curious Gentiles.
    D. with many of Jesus' followers.

3. **By approaching the group, Jesus**
    A. showed His curiosity about who had sought Him out.
    B. demonstrated His willingness to go to the cross and His control of the situation.
    C. planned to defend Himself from capture.
    D. deflected Judas' intention to betray Him.

4. **When Jesus said He was _____, the arresting company fell to the ground.**
    A. Jesus, the son of Mary
    C. the miracle worker
    B. Jesus of Nazareth
    D. the I AM

5. **Peter tried to defend Jesus by striking _____ with a sword.**
    A. Judas
    C. the high priest's servant
    B. the high priest
    D. the Roman guard

6. **What was the practical lesson the author drew from Peter's warming himself at the fire inside the courtyard?**
    A. In order to witness to unbelievers we have to meet them on their ground.
    B. We should not be afraid to get close to those who are hostile to Christ.
    C. There is spiritual danger in warming oneself at the world's fire.
    D. Take every opportunity you can to get close to the Lord.

EXAM 10

7. **The high priest Annas questioned Jesus concerning**
   A. His disciples and His teaching.
   B. His power to work miracles.
   C. His birth and childhood.
   D. His political aspirations.

8. **Why did the Jewish leaders refuse to enter Pilate's palace?**
   A. They feared a plot against them.
   B. The Law forbade any contact with Gentiles.
   C. They wanted to show their authority.
   D. Doing so would defile them.

9. **What prophecies given by Jesus were fulfilled by His being turned over to the Romans?**
   A. His being crucified by the Gentiles.
   B. His disciples being kept from physical harm at that time.
   C. The destruction of Jerusalem.
   D. His rejection by the Jews.

10. **Pilate declared that**
    A. Jesus was guilty of sedition.
    B. he found no fault in Him at all.
    C. Jesus should be held for further investigation.
    D. Jesus was free to go.

What Do You Say?

Which divine attributes of the Lord Jesus are evident in this chapter?

LESSON 11

Jesus Dies for the World

John 19

"Away with Him! Crucify Him!" (19:1-16)

Having released Barabbas, Pilate now had the Lord Jesus scourged. Scourging was a Roman form of punishment where the prisoner was beaten with a whip or rod. Often the whip had pieces of metal or bone in it, and these cut deep gashes in the flesh. It was most unjust of Pilate to scourge an innocent person. Perhaps he hoped that this punishment would satisfy the Jews and that they would not demand him to execute Jesus.

The Lord Jesus wore a crown of thorns so that we might wear a crown of glory.

The soldiers mocked Jesus' claim to be a king by making him a crown, a crown of thorns. This would have been extremely painful when pressed onto His brow. If we view thorns as symbolizing the curse which sin brought to mankind (cf. Gen. 3:18), we have here a picture of the Lord Jesus bearing the curse of our sins so that we might go free. He wore a crown of thorns so that we might wear a crown of glory. The purple robe was also used to mock Him. Purple was the color of royalty. Our sins were placed on Jesus that we might be clothed with the robe of God's righteousness. How solemn it is to think of the eternal Son of God being slapped by the hands of His creatures and being mocked by mouths He had formed!

Pilate went out to the Jews and announced he would bring Jesus to them, but that He was innocent (19:4). Thus Pilate condemned himself by his own words. He found no fault in Christ, yet he would not let Him go. As Jesus came forth wearing the crown of thorns and the purple robe, Pilate announced Him as "the Man." It is difficult to know whether he said this in mockery, in sympathy, or without any particular emotion. The chief priests took this moment to cry out fiercely for Jesus to be crucified. It was religious men who were leaders in the death of their Messiah. Often, down through the centuries, it has been church officials who have most bitterly persecuted true believers.

Pilate Tries to Negotiate with the Jews

Pilate seemed to be disgusted with them and with their unreasonable hatred of Jesus. He said in effect: "If that is the way you feel, why don't you take Him and crucify Him? As far as I am concerned, He is innocent." He knew, however, that the Jews could not put Him to death without his consent. When the Jews saw they had failed to prove Jesus to be a threat to Caesar's government, they brought forth their religious charge (19:7). Christ claimed equality with God by saying that He was the Son of God. To the Jews this was blasphemy and should be punished by death. The possibility of Jesus being Deity troubled Pilate. From verse 8 we see that he was already uneasy about the whole affair, but this made him more afraid. He took Jesus into the judgment hall (or palace) and asked Him who He was and where He came from. Pilate is a tragic figure! He confessed that Jesus had done no wrong, yet because he feared the Jews, he did not have the moral courage to let Him go.

Jesus refused to answer him. He knew Pilate was unwilling to do what he knew to be right. He would be given no more light, for he had not responded to the light he had. This is a sobering principle we observe throughout Scripture. Pilate tried to force Jesus to answer by threatening Him. In verse 10 he reminded Jesus that, as Roman governor, he had the authority to set Him free or to put Him to death. Jesus' self-control was remarkable—He was calmer than Pilate! He answered that whatever authority Pilate had, it was given to him by God. All governments are ordained by God, and all power, whether civil or spiritual, is from God. "The one who delivered Me to you has the greater sin," He said. This may refer to Caiaphas, the high priest, to Judas, the betrayer, or to the Jewish people in general. The thought is that these Jews should have known better. They had the Scriptures, which predicted

> **All governments are ordained by God, and all power, whether civil or spiritual, is from God.**

Messiah's coming. They should have recognized Him when He came. But they rejected Him and were even now demanding His death. This verse teaches us that there are degrees of guilt; Pilate was guilty, but Caiaphas, Judas, and all the wicked Jews were even more guilty.

Pilate Submits to the Jews

We see in verse 12 that just as Pilate was making up his mind to let Jesus go, the Jews used their last and most telling argument: "If you let this Man go, you are not Caesar's friend." As if they cared for the Roman emperor! They hated him. They would have destroyed him if they had been able, and freed themselves from his control. Yet they pretended to protect Caesar's empire from the threat of this Jesus who claimed to be a king! They reaped the punishment of this hypocrisy when in AD 70 the Romans marched into Jerusalem and destroyed the city and slaughtered its inhabitants. Pilate could not afford to have the Jews accuse him of disloyalty to Caesar, so he weakly submitted to the mob and brought Jesus forth to an outdoor area called the Pavement.

The Passover feast had been held the previous evening. The "preparation of the Passover" mentioned now refers to the preparation for the Feast that followed it (19:14). It was "about the sixth hour." Mark says that it was the third hour (Mark 15:25). Probably Mark used the Jewish method of telling time, whereas John used the Roman method. "Behold your King!" said Pilate, almost certainly to annoy and provoke the Jews. He no doubt blamed them for trapping him so that he had to condemn Jesus to death. But the Jews were insisting that Jesus must be crucified. Pilate taunted them with the question, "Shall I crucify your King?" Then the Jews stooped by saying, "We have no king but Caesar." Their reply was a remarkable fulfillment of Genesis 49:10: "The scepter shall not depart from Judah … until Shiloh comes." By their own admission, the scepter, or government, had departed from the nation. But their words also demonstrated that Shiloh, the Rest-Giver, had come—and this was the very thing they refused to believe. "We have no king but Caesar," they cried. Faithless nation! Pilate, wanting to pacify the Jews, turned Jesus over to the soldiers to be crucified. He loved the praise of men more than the praise of God.

"What I have written, I have written" (19:17-24)

The cross may have been a single piece of wood or it may have been two cross pieces. At any rate, it was of such size that a man could carry it.

Jesus carried His own cross for some distance. Then, according to the other gospels, it was given to a man named Simon of Cyrene to carry. "The place of a skull," where Christ was crucified, may have received its name in one of two ways. It was the place where criminals were executed, and perhaps skulls and bones were often found in the area. Or perhaps the land itself may have resembled a skull, especially if it was a hill with caves in the side of it.

The Lord Jesus was nailed to the cross by His hands and feet. The cross would have been lifted up and dropped into a hole in the ground. Two thieves were crucified with Him, one on His left and one on His right. This fulfilled the prophecy of Isaiah 53:12: "He was numbered with the transgressors." If you have not yet trusted Him as your Lord and Savior, will you do it now, as you read this simple account of how He died for you?

It was the custom to put a title above the head of the crucified one to publicize his crime, and Pilate ordered that the title JESUS OF NAZARETH, THE KING OF THE JEWS be placed on the center cross. It was written in Hebrew, Greek, and Latin. Alexander comments,

> In Hebrew, the sacred tongue of patriarchs and seers. In Greek, the musical and golden tongue which gave a soul to the objects of sense and a body to the abstractions of philosophy. In Latin, the dialect of a people originally the strongest of all the sons of men. The three languages represent the three races and their ideas—revelation, art, literature; progress, war, and jurisprudence. Wherever these three desires of the human race exist, wherever annunciation can be made in human language, wherever there is a heart to sin, a tongue to speak, an eye to read, the Cross has a message.

"The place," we are told, "was near the city." Jesus was crucified outside the city limits, but as to the exact location, it is no longer known for certain. From verse 21 we learn that the chief priests did not like the wording. They wanted it to read as a *claim* made by Jesus, but not as a *fact*. Pilate refused to change the writing, and in doing so he bore testimony to the truth. He had become impatient with the Jews and would not give in to them any more. But he should have shown this determination sooner!

At such executions, the soldiers were allowed to share among themselves the personal effects of those who died. Here in verse 23 we find them parceling out Christ's garments. Apparently there were five pieces altogether. They divided four, but there remained the coat (or tunic), which was seamless and could not be cut up without ruining it. They cast lots for this, and it was handed over to the unnamed winner. Little did they know they were fulfilling a prophecy written a thousand years before (Ps. 22:18). These fulfilled prophecies remind us afresh that this Book is the inspired Word of God, and that Jesus Christ is indeed the promised Messiah.

"Woman, behold your son! ... Behold your mother!" (19:25-27)

Many think there are four women named in verse 25—Mary, the mother of Jesus; Mary's sister, Salome, the mother of John; Mary, the wife of Cleophas; and Mary Magdalene. In spite of His own suffering, Jesus had tender regard for others. Seeing His mother, and John, the disciple, He pointed out John as the one who would take the place of son to her from that point on. Constable says, "John was Jesus' cousin on His mother's side. As such, he was a logical person to assume responsibility for Mary's welfare." In calling His mother "Woman," Jesus showed no disrespect, but it is worth noting that He did not call her "Mother." This surely is a lesson for those who might be tempted to exalt Mary to the place where she is adored. Jesus here instructed John to take care of Mary as if she were his own mother. John obeyed and took Mary to his own home.

> In spite of His own suffering, Jesus had tender regard for others.

"It is finished!" (19:28-30)

Between verses 27 and 28 probably transpired the three hours of darkness—from noon to 3:00 pm. It was during this time that Jesus Christ was forsaken by God as He suffered the penalty of our sins. His cry, "I thirst," indicated real, physical thirst, which had been intensified by crucifixion. The soldiers gave Him sour wine (like vinegar) to drink. They tied the sponge to the end of a rod with hyssop and pressed it to His lips. (Hyssop was a plant, also used at the Passover, Exodus 12:22.) This act is not to be confused with the vinegar mingled with gall which had been offered to Him earlier (Matt. 27:34). He had refused that because it was a pain-killing drug; He must bear our sins in full consciousness.

In verse 30 we read of the great cry of the Lord: "It is finished!" He had completed the work His Father had given Him to do! He had poured out His soul as an offering for sin! In those three hours of darkness He had borne condemnation from God for all our sin! The work of redemption and of atonement was complete! It is true He had not died physically as yet, but His death, burial, and ascension were as certain as if already accomplished. So He announced the way was open for sinners to be saved. Thank God for the finished work of the Lord Jesus on the cross of Calvary! In the phrase "bowing His head," some say He leaned His head backward. "Not the helpless dropping of the head after death," says Vine, "but the deliberate putting of His head into a position of rest." And then "He gave up His spirit." His death was voluntary. He determined its time. In full control of His faculties, He dismissed His spirit—an act no mere man could accomplish.

"One of the soldiers pierced His side with a spear" (19:31-37)

In verse 31, we see again how careful these religious Jews were about details even while they were murdering their Messiah. They couldn't allow the bodies to remain on the cross on the Sabbath day (Saturday) as they were about to celebrate a religious feast in the city, so they requested Pilate to have the legs of the three victims broken to hasten death. We are not told how the legs were broken. However, they must have been broken in many different places, since a single break would not bring on death. The soldiers were well experienced in such matters.

> **Thank God for the finished work of the Lord Jesus on the cross of Calvary!**

When they came to Jesus, they found that He was dead already (19:33). In verse 34 they made sure: "But one of the soldiers pierced His side with a spear, and immediately blood and water came out." Perhaps this was a final outburst of wickedness.

Constable notes that the flow of blood and water from the Lord's side indicates that "the spear had entered the body near the bottom of the chest cavity [piercing the surrounding pericardial sac that contains water]. Apparently the soldier pierced Jesus' side before His blood congealed into a solid. The eyewitness testimony stresses the fact that Jesus really did die and that He was a genuine man (cf. 1:14)." Constable goes on to point out that John's inclusion of this detail may have been designed to thwart some false teachings about Christ: "By the end of the first century, when John probably wrote this gospel, Docetism and Gnosticism were on the rise. Both of these heresies denied that Jesus was a real man."

Verse 35 may refer to the fact that Jesus' legs were not broken, or to the piercing of Jesus' side, or to the entire crucifixion scene. "He who has seen has testified" undoubtedly refers to John, who wrote the account. Verse 36 looks back to verse 33 as a fulfillment of Exodus 12:46: "Nor shall you break one of its bones," referring to the Passover lamb. God's decree was that the bones of the lamb were to be maintained unbroken. Christ is the true Passover Lamb, fulfilling the "type" exactly. Verse 37 looks back to verse 34. Although the soldier did not realize it, his act was a fulfillment of Zechariah 12:10. This prophecy also refers to a future day when believing Jews will see the Lord coming back. "They will look on Me whom they pierced. Yes, they will mourn for Him as one mourns for his only son."

"So there they laid Jesus" (19:38-42)

Now begins the account of the burial of Jesus. Up until now, Joseph of Arimathea had been a secret believer. Fear of the Jews had kept him from confessing his allegiance to Christ openly. Now he boldly stepped forward to claim Christ's body for burial. In doing this, he exposed himself to excommunication, persecution, and violence. It is only regrettable that he was not willing to take his stand for a rejected Master while Jesus was still living. Nicodemus came too. We have met him before—in chapter 3 when he came to Jesus by night, and in chapter 7 when he urged that Jesus be given a fair hearing before the Sanhedrin. He now joined Joseph, bringing with him a hundred-pound weight of spices. The spices were probably in powdered form and were spread on the body. Then the body was bound with linen cloth.

Almost every detail fulfilled a prophecy. Isaiah had predicted that men would plan to bury the Messiah with the wicked but that He would be with the rich in His death (Isa. 53:9). A sepulcher in a garden would obviously belong to a rich man. In Matthew's gospel, we learn that the tomb belonged to Joseph. The body of Jesus was laid in the tomb. The Jews were anxious to have the body out of the way because of their feast that began at sunset. But it was all part of God's plan that the body should be in the heart of the earth for three days and three nights. In Jewish reckoning, any part of a day was counted as a day. So the fact that the Lord was in the sepulcher for a part of three days still fulfilled His prediction in Matthew 12:40.

LESSON 11 EXAM

Use the answer sheet that has been provided to complete your exam.

1. **The soldiers _____ Jesus by giving Him a crown and a purple robe.**
   A. mocked
   C. exalted
   B. praised
   D. punished

2. **Because the Jews failed to convince Pilate that Jesus was a threat to the Romans,**
   A. they asked that He be sent to Herod for judgment.
   B. they grabbed Him and stoned Him.
   C. they accused Him of blasphemy.
   D. they brought many witnesses against Him.

3. **Pilate's ultimate authority over Jesus came from**
   A. Caesar.
   C. the people.
   B. God.
   D. the Jews.

4. **Pilate capitulated to the will of the Jews when the Jews said,**
   A. "If you let this Man go, we will send a delegation to Caesar to report you."
   B. "If you let this Man go, we will cause a large scale riot in the city."
   C. "If you let this Man go, you are an unjust judge."
   D. "If you let this Man go, you are not Caesar's friend."

5. **Jesus was crucified with two thieves. This fulfilled the prophecy of**
   A. Genesis 49:10.
   C. Psalm 22:10.
   B. Exodus 12:46.
   D. Isaiah 53:12.

6. **The title written over Jesus' cross was**
   A. Jesus of Nazareth, the King of the Jews.
   B. Jesus of Nazareth, the Prophet from Galilee.
   C. Jesus of Nazareth, the Miracle Worker.
   D. Jesus of Nazareth, the Son of God.

7. **Jesus gave His mother into the care of**
   A. His half-brother, James.
   B. the whole group of disciples.
   C. the apostle John.
   D. the apostle Peter.

8. **When Jesus had fully paid the price for our redemption, He cried out, "It is finished" and**
   A. went immediately to heaven.
   B. dismissed His spirit.
   C. said goodbye to His disciples.
   D. told Satan he was now defeated.

9. **The soldiers were instructed to break the legs of those crucified in order to hasten their death. Why were Jesus' legs not broken?**
   A. He begged them not to.
   B. He was already dead.
   C. The soldiers had compassion on Him.
   D. His disciples threatened the soldiers.

10. **The place of the burial of the Lord Jesus**
    A. was ordered by the Jewish leaders.
    B. fulfilled prophecy.
    C. was strongly contested by Caiaphas.
    D. has no significance.

EXAM 11

What Do You Say?

Write a prayer of personal response to Christ's suffering and death.

Jesus Is Raised and Appears to His Disciples

John 20–21

"The stone had been taken away from the tomb" (20:1-10)

"The first day of the week" was Sunday. Mary Magdalene came to the sepulcher before dawn. The sepulcher was probably a small room carved in the side of a hill or cliff. The stone was no doubt shaped like a coin—round and flat. It would fit into a groove or gutter along the front of the sepulcher and could be rolled across the opening to close it. When Mary arrived, the stone had already been removed. This, incidentally, had taken place *after* Christ's resurrection, as we learn in Matthew 28. Mary immediately ran to Peter and John with the breathless announcement that someone had removed the Lord's body from the sepulcher. She did not say who had done it but just said "they" to indicate that this was all she knew. The faithfulness and devotion of women at the crucifixion and resurrection of our Lord should be noticed. The disciples had forsaken Jesus and fled; the women stood by without regard for their personal safety. These things are not without meaning.

We don't know what Peter and John were thinking as they hurried out of the city to the garden near Calvary. John was probably younger than Peter and reached the empty tomb first. It is likely there was a low opening to the tomb, requiring them to stoop to enter or to look in. John saw the linen cloths lying there, probably still in the general shape in which they had been wrapped around the body. In verse 5 we see that John did not enter the tomb. By now Peter had caught up, and in his usual impulsive manner entered the sepulcher without hesitation. He too saw the linen cloths, but the body of the Savior was not there. The detail John gives in verse 7 shows that the Lord's departure was orderly and unhurried; if someone had stolen the body, he would not have bothered to fold the handkerchief that had been wrapped around Christ's head. John followed Peter into the tomb and saw the orderly arrangement of the linen and the handkerchief. "He *saw* and *believed*"—that is, he comprehended. Before him were the evidences of Christ's resurrection. The Lord Himself had told them repeatedly, but they did not take it in. John was the first to understand. Peter and John returned to their lodgings, probably in Jerusalem. There was no point in waiting by the tomb; it would be better to tell the other disciples what they had found.

"Woman, why are you weeping?" (20:11-18)

The first two words of verse 11 are striking—"But Mary." The other two disciples went home, *but Mary* ... Here again we have the love and devotion of a woman. She had been forgiven much, therefore she loved much. She kept a lonely vigil outside the tomb, weeping because, as she thought, her Lord's body had been stolen, probably by His enemies. Then she looked inside and saw two angels stationed where the body had lain. It is remarkable how these tremendous facts are stated quietly and without great emotion. She still did not realize that Jesus had risen and was alive again.

At this point, something caused her to look behind her (20:14). It was Jesus Himself, but she did not recognize Him. It was still early in the morning, and perhaps light had not yet dawned. She had been weeping continually, and obviously was greatly upset. Also, perhaps God prevented her from recognizing the Lord until the proper time came. The Lord, knowing well the answer, asked her why she wept. He wanted to hear from her own lips the reason for her distress. She assumed He was the gardener. Mary did not name the Lord. Three times she referred to Jesus as "Him." There was only one person with whom she was concerned, and she felt it quite unnecessary to identify Him further.

Mary now heard a familiar voice calling her by name (20:16). There was no mistaking—it was Jesus! She called Him "Rabboni," which means "my Great Teacher." She was still thinking of Him as the Great Teacher she had known. She did not realize that He was now more than her Teacher— He was her Lord and her Savior. So the Lord must explain to her the newer and fuller way in which she would hereafter know Him. "Do not cling to Me," He said (20:17). This does not mean that Mary should not even touch His body with her fingers. It means, "Do not hold onto Me." Mary had known Jesus as a man in the flesh. She had seen miracles happen when He was physically present. So she concluded that if He wasn't physically present, then she could have no hope of blessing.

The Lord had to correct her thinking. "Do not cling to Me simply as a man in the flesh," He was saying. "I have not yet ascended to My Father. When I do return to heaven, the Holy Spirit will be sent down to the earth. When He comes, He will reveal Me to your heart in a way you have never known Me before. I will be nearer and dearer to you than was possible during My life here." Then He told her to go to the disciples and tell them of the new order that had been ushered in. For the first time, the Lord referred to the disciples as "My brethren." They were to know that His Father was their Father, and His God was their God. The Lord did not say, "Our Father." God is His Father in a different sense than He is ours. God is the Father of the Lord Jesus Christ from all eternity. Christ is the Son by eternal generation. The Son is equal with the Father; *we* are sons of God by adoption. It is a relationship that begins when we are saved—and it will never end. As sons of God, we are not equal with God and never shall be. Mary obeyed His commission and became, as it were, "the apostle to the apostles." This great privilege was no doubt given her as a reward for her devotion to Christ.

> **We are sons of God by adoption. It is a relationship that begins when we are saved—and it will never end.**

"When the doors were shut … Jesus came" (20:19-23)

In verse 19 we come to Sunday evening. The disciples were gathered together, perhaps in the upper room where they had met three nights earlier. The doors were locked because they feared the Jewish leaders would arrest them too. Suddenly they saw Jesus standing in their midst and heard Him say, "Peace." The Lord entered the room without opening the doors. His resurrection body was a real body of flesh and bones, yet He had the power to pass through barriers and act independently of natural laws. "Peace be with you," He said. These words now have new meaning because Christ has made peace by the blood of His cross. Those who are justified by faith have peace with God (Rom. 5:1). Then in verse 20 He showed them the marks of His passion, marks that demonstrated something of what He had endured to obtain for man peace with God. They saw the prints of the nails and the spear wound. Joy filled their hearts—it was truly the Lord! He had done as He said; He had risen from the dead.

But the Lord's disciples were not meant to enjoy His peace selfishly—they must share it with others. So He sent them into the world, just as the Father had sent Him. Christ came into the world as a poor person; He came as a Servant; He emptied Himself; He delighted to do the Father's will; He identified Himself with man; He went about doing good; He did everything by the power of the Holy Spirit; His goal was the cross. Now He said to His disciples, "I also send you."

Verse 22 reads this way: "And when He had said this, He breathed on them, and said to them, 'Receive the Holy Spirit.'" This is one of the most difficult verses in the gospel to interpret, and we cannot resolve it here. The difficulty is that the Holy Spirit was not given until the day of Pentecost, so how could the Lord speak these words without the event taking place immediately? Several explanations have been offered. Some suggest the Lord was making a *promise* of what they would receive on the day of Pentecost; this is hardly adequate. Some point out that what Christ actually said was, "Receive Holy Spirit," not "Receive *the* Holy Spirit." They conclude from this that the disciples did not receive *the* Holy Spirit in all His fullness at this time, but only some ministry of the Spirit, such as a greater knowledge of the truth, or power and guidance for their mission. They say that the disciples received a foretaste of the Holy Spirit. Others state that there was a full outpouring of the Holy Spirit upon the disciples at this time. This seems unlikely in view of Luke 24:49 and Acts 1:4-5, 8, where the coming of the Holy Spirit was still spoken of as future. It is clear from John 7:39 that the Spirit could not come in His fullness until Jesus was glorified, that is, until He had gone back to heaven.

Verse 23 is difficult too, and has been the source of much controversy. One view is that Jesus actually gave His apostles (and their supposed successors) the power to forgive or retain sins. This is in direct contradiction

> The Lord's disciples were not meant to enjoy His peace selfishly—they must share it with others.

of the Bible teaching that only God can forgive sins (Luke 5:21). A second view is that the power promised and authority given is in connection with the preaching of the gospel, announcing on what terms sins would be forgiven, and that if these terms are not accepted, sins would be retained. A third view, and the one that we accept, is that the disciples were given the right to *declare* sins forgiven. For example, the disciples go forth preaching the gospel; some people repent of their sins and receive the Lord Jesus; the disciples are authorized to tell them that their sins have been forgiven. Others refuse to repent and will not believe on Christ; the disciples tell them that they are still in their sins, and that if they die, they will perish eternally.

Note also that the disciples were given special authority by the Lord in dealing with certain sins. Peter used this power in Acts 5:1-11, and it resulted in the death of Ananias and Sapphira. Paul is seen retaining the sin of an evil-doer in 1 Corinthians 5:3-5, 12-13, and remitting that same sin in 2 Corinthians 2:4-8. In these cases, it is forgiveness from the punishment of these sins *in this life, not eternal punishment.*

"Blessed are those who have not seen and yet have believed" (20:24-29)

"Thomas, called the Twin, one of the twelve, was not with them when Jesus came." We should not blame Thomas for not being present as we do not know why he was absent. But Thomas *is* to be blamed for his unbelieving attitude. He wanted visible, tangible proof of the Lord's resurrection, otherwise he would not believe. This is the attitude of many today, but it is not reasonable. We believe in many things we can neither see nor touch.

In verse 26 it is one week later, and Jesus appeared to the disciples again. This time Thomas was present. Again Jesus entered the room in a miraculous way, and again He greeted them with "Peace." The Lord dealt gently and patiently with doubting Thomas. He invited him to prove the reality of His resurrection by thrusting his hand into the spear wound. In verse 28 we see that Thomas was convinced. Whether he ever did put his hand into Jesus' side, we do not know. But he knew at last that Jesus was risen and that He was both Lord and God—*his* Lord and God. Notice that Jesus accepted worship as God. If He were a mere man, He should have refused it. But Thomas's faith was not the kind that was most pleasing to the Lord—it was belief based on sight. More blessed are those who have never seen and yet have believed.

"These are written that you may believe" (20:30-31)

Not all the miracles performed by Jesus are recorded in John's gospel. The Holy Spirit inspired John to select those which would best serve His purpose. John now states his object in writing the book. It was written that the readers might believe that Jesus is the true Christ and the Son of God. By believing, they will have eternal life through Him. Have you placed your faith in Him?

"It is the Lord!" (21:1-14)

In chapter 21 the scene changes to the Sea of Galilee. The disciples have journeyed north to their homes in Galilee. The Lord Jesus meets them there. Seven of the disciples were together at the time—Peter, Thomas, Nathanael, James and John (the two sons of Zebedee), and two unnamed ones. Peter decided to go fishing on the lake, and the others agreed to go with him. That night they caught nothing. They were not the first fishermen to spend a night fishing without success; they illustrate the uselessness of human efforts apart from divine help, especially in the matter of fishing for souls.

In verse 4 we see Jesus waiting for them as they rowed toward the shore in the morning. They did not recognize Him; perhaps it was still quite dark, or perhaps God prevented them from knowing Him. "Then Jesus said to them, 'Children, have you any food?' They answered him, 'No.'" As far as they knew, He was just a stranger walking along the shore. Yet they cast the net on the right side of the boat at His command and, behold, a great catch of fish—so many, they could not pull in the net!

> The "sign" of the miraculous draught of fish is not to be confused with a similar miracle wrought by our Lord at the opening of his ministry [Luke 5:1-11]; it is, however, to be interpreted in light of that previous event. On that former occasion Jesus stated clearly the truth he wished to illustrate: "Come ye after me, and I will make you fishers of men." So now it required no word of explanation to impress upon his disciples the truth that he had called them to undertake for him the work of "saving men alive."
>
> –Charles Erdman

Jesus had perfect knowledge where the fish were in the lake. Similarly, He directs our service and there are no more empty nets. He knows where there are souls ready to be saved, and He is willing to direct us to them—if we heed His leading.

John (21:7) is the first to recognize the Lord. He promptly told Peter, who at once put on his fisherman's coat and made his way to the shore. The other disciples transferred from the large fishing boat to a small rowboat and dragged the net around three hundred feet to land. Jesus had some breakfast all ready—one broiled fish and some bread.

> Even though there was already one "fish" (Greek, singular) on the fire, Jesus instructed the disciples to "bring some of the fish" (plural) they had "caught." He would not provide for their physical needs by multiplying the food miraculously, as He had done in the past. Now He would use the product of their labor to satisfy their need. Nevertheless it was clear that their fish had been the result of His miraculous provision. Perhaps this was all symbolic of how Jesus would carry out His mission through His disciples in the future, compared with how He had done it during His pre-cross ministry.
>
> –Thomas Constable

Addressing the recording of the exact number of fish caught (153 large ones), Leon Morris comments: "It seems probable that he says this for no more profound reason than that this was the actual number that was caught … Since the catch was presumably to be shared among the fishermen, it was necessary to count the fish preparatory to assigning shares."

The fishermen knew it was remarkable that the net had not broken. This is further evidence that God's work carried on in God's way will never lack God's resources. He will ensure that the net does not break; this "may symbolize the capability of the gospel to 'catch' many people without failing" (F. F. Bruce).

The invitation to breakfast is given in verse 12, and the disciples gather around the fire of coals to partake of the good things the Lord had provided. Peter must have had his own thoughts as he saw the fire of coals; did they remind him of the fire at which he warmed himself when he denied any association with Jesus? The disciples must have felt a strange sense of awe and solemnity in the presence of their Lord. There He stood in His resurrection body. No doubt there were many questions they would have liked to ask Him—but they did not dare. They knew it was Jesus, even if they felt a certain sense of mystery shrouded His person.

"This is now the third time," John says in verse 14, "Jesus showed Himself to His disciples after He was raised from the dead." This was the third time mentioned by John, that is. It is clear from the other gospels that Jesus appeared to them on several other occasions. John records His appearing to the disciples on the evening of the day of the resurrection, then one week later, and now by the shore of the Sea of Galilee.

"Simon ... do you love Me more than these?" (21:15-17)

The Lord first took care of their physical needs. Then, when they were warm and had eaten, He turned to Peter and dealt with spiritual matters. Peter had publicly denied his association with Christ three times. Since then, he had repented and had been restored to fellowship with the Lord. In these verses, Christ publicly acknowledges Peter's restoration.

In responding to the Lord's probing question, Peter would no longer boast that even if all the other disciples forsook the Lord, he never would. He had learned his lesson. "Feed my lambs," said Jesus. He "responded graciously by giving Peter a command, not a criticism" (Constable). A very practical way of demonstrating love for Christ is by feeding the young ones in His flock. Note the conversation had changed from fishing to shepherding. The former speaks of the work of evangelism; the latter suggests teaching and pastoral care.

For the second time, Jesus asked Peter if he loved Him. Peter replied again the same way. This time the Lord told him, "Feed my sheep." There are lambs and sheep in Christ's flock, and they need the loving care of one who loves the Shepherd.

As Peter had denied the Lord three times, so he was given three opportunities to confess Him. "Peter had learned not to make rash professions of great love. Therefore he did not compare his love for Jesus to the love of the other disciples, as he had done before. He simply appealed to Jesus' knowledge of his heart" (Constable). And for the last time, Jesus told him he could demonstrate his love by feeding Christ's sheep. In this passage, the underlying lesson is that love for Christ is the only acceptable motive for serving Him, and it is what He most desires from us.

"Follow Me … You follow Me" (21:18-23)

As a young man, Peter had enjoyed great freedom to come and go where he wanted. But now, Jesus told him that, at the end of his life, he would be arrested, bound, and carried off to execution (21:19). He would glorify God by dying as a martyr. He who had denied the Lord would be given courage to lay down his life for Him. We can glorify God in death as well as in life. Then Jesus said, "Follow Me!"

As He said this, He must have started to leave. It seems from verse 20 that Peter began to follow Him, and then turned and saw John following too. Here John paused to identify himself as the one who leaned on Jesus' breast at the Passover supper and asked the name of the betrayer. As Peter saw John, the thought crossed his mind, "What about John? Is he going to die as a martyr too? Or will he still be alive when the Lord comes back again?" He asked the Lord concerning John's future (21:21). The answer he got was to not be concerned about John's end. Even if he were to survive until the second coming of Christ, this should not make any difference to Peter.

Many failures in Christian service arise from disciples being more occupied with one another than with the Lord

> Love for Christ is the only acceptable motive for serving Him, and it is what He most desires from us.

Himself. The Lord's words were later misquoted by others. He did not say that John would still be alive when He came back. He only said that if such were the case, why should it affect Peter? Jesus here linked John with His second advent. John, incidentally, was the one who wrote the book of Revelation, describing the end times in great detail. It was in his final years, when he was returned to Ephesus following his enforced exile on the Island of Patmos, that we believe he penned this gospel and the three letters included in our Bible entitled 1, 2, and 3 John.

"There are also many other things that Jesus did" (21:24-25)

John now added a word of personal testimony to the accuracy of the things that he had written. Then he said, "And there are also many other things that Jesus did, which if they were written one by one, I suppose that even the world itself could not contain the books that would be written. Amen." We can take this literally. Jesus is God and is therefore infinite.

There is no limit to the meaning of His words or to the number of His works. While He was on earth, He was still the Upholder of all things—the sun, the moon, the stars. Who could ever describe all that is involved in keeping the universe in motion? We have only the barest description even of His miracles on earth. In a simple act of healing, think of the nerves, muscles, blood cells, and other members that He controlled. Think of His direction of germs, fish, animal life. Think of His guidance in the affairs of people and nations. Think of His control over the atomic structure of every bit of matter in the universe. Would the world itself contain the books to describe such infinite details? The answer is an emphatic no.

And so we come to the end of our studies in John's gospel. Perhaps we realize a little better now why it has come to be one of the most beloved portions of the Bible. Certainly we can scarcely read it thoughtfully and prayerfully without growing in awe, worship, and devotion to the blessed person it presents: the Lord Jesus Christ, the Son of God.

LESSON 12 EXAM

Use the answer sheet that has been provided to complete your exam.

1. **Those who were most faithful in standing by the Lord when He was on the cross were**
    A. the women.
    B. the disciples as a whole.
    C. people who had been healed by Him.
    D. Gentile admirers.

2. **John's conclusion in believing Christ had risen from the dead was partly due to**
    A. the absence of any smell of decay in the tomb.
    B. the presence of 2 angels in the tomb.
    C. the orderly state of the grave clothes that had been left behind.
    D. Peter's convincing him of it.

3. **Christ's command to Mary not to cling to Him conveyed**
    A. He didn't want to be close to her anymore.
    B. it wasn't appropriate for them to touch each other when they were alone.
    C. as He was no longer flesh and blood, He would "feel" different now.
    D. their future relationship would be of a heavenly and spiritual nature.

4. **What convinced His disciples that Jesus truly had risen from the dead?**
    A. He appeared to them without opening the locked door.
    B. Mary told them that she had seen Him.
    C. They put their fingers in the nail prints in His hands.
    D. They heard a voice from heaven declaring He had risen.

5. **Jesus gave His followers the authority to**
    A. forgive people's sins.
    B. declare who should be sent to hell.
    C. declare forgiveness of sins to anyone who believed the gospel.
    D. decide which sins are forgivable and which are not.

EXAM 12

6. **When the Lord appeared to the disciples in the upper room the second time, He**
   A. rebuked Thomas severely for his unbelief.
   B. commended Thomas for his healthy skepticism.
   C. told Thomas he would be an example of faith.
   D. dealt gently with Thomas about his unbelief.

7. **Jesus commended those who**
   A. believe in Him without any basis for doing so.
   B. desire to see Him in order to believe in Him.
   C. believe in Him without seeing Him.
   D. preach blind faith in Him.

8. **John's purpose in writing this book was**
   A. that there would be a complete record of all Jesus had said and done.
   B. that he could give an accurate history of the time he spent with Jesus.
   C. that he could justify the martyrdom of Jesus' disciples.
   D. that people would believe Jesus was the Christ, and by believing have life in His name.

9. **In the exchange between the Lord and Peter, "the underlying lesson is that _____ is the only acceptable motive for serving Him, and it is what He most desires from us."**
   A. wanting to be a leader
   B. love for Christ
   C. destroying Satan's control over people
   D. a heart for the lost

10. **The Lord told Peter he would**
    A. live longer than all the other disciples.
    B. be a martyr for Him.
    C. die a natural death.
    D. stay alive until He returned.

What Do You Say?

How do you plan to implement one of the practical principles/exhortations given in this final lesson?

_____

_____

_____

_____

And this is eternal life, that they may know You, the only true God, and Jesus Christ whom You have sent.

—John 17:3